How to
Be Filled
with *Spiritual*
Power

How to
Be Filled
with Spiritual
Power

Based on the Miracle Ministry of
John G. Lake

By Harold J. Chadwick

Bridge-Logos
Gainesville, Florida

Bridge-Logos

Gainesville, FL 32614 USA

How to Be Filled with Spiritual Power
by Harold J. Chadwick

Library of Congress Catalog Card Number: 2005939119
International Standard Book Number 0-88270-098-7

Unless otherwise indicated, the Scripture quotations in this publication are from The New King James Version. Copyright ©1979, 1980, 1982, Thomas Nelson Inc., Publishers. Used by permission.

Scripture quotations marked (AMP) are taken from The Amplified Bible, Old Testament. Copyright ©1965, 1987 by The Zondervan Corporation. The Amplified New Testament, copyright ©1954, 1958, 1987 by The Lockman Foundation. Used by permission.

Scripture quotations marked KJV are from the King James Version of the Bible. Most of the Scriptures quoted in John G. Lake's material are from the KJV.

The Healer: Dr. John G. Lake is Chapter 15 of Let the Light Shine Out: The Story of the Assemblies of God in the Pacific Northwest by Ward M. Tanneberg, Ph.D., used by permission of the author.

Editorial insertions into original material are enclosed in [brackets].

G1.316.N.m601.35230

Dedication

This book is dedicated with love to my wife, Beverlee, who has been my companion and friend for over fifty years.

It is also dedicated to our children: Kimberlee, Hollee, Steve, Barbara, and Thomas — may Jesus Christ always be as important in their lives as He is in ours.

Thanks

My special thanks to Al and Ruth Webber for their help in researching the material for this book — they are blessed friends in the Lord.

Many years ago the Lord gave Beverlee and me a true and loyal friend, one whose heart has never wavered from us through many ups and downs — there is no better gift the Lord could give, and no better friend than Jeffrey R. Fryman. Thank you, Jeff, for being our friend.

My thanks also to Bill Funck, Cindy Volz, Geneive Garwood, Patrick Becus, Roger Smith, and Al and Ruth for listening to me every Sunday afternoon without hardly ever cringing.

Contents

Preface

It's a rare Christian who would not want the kind of spiritual power that John G. Lake had, even if it was only for a few months or a few years.

Power of any kind is exhilarating and exciting, but spiritual power that manifests itself in the healing of sick bodies and minds and the salvation of lost souls is a joyous gift of God that contains within it the joy of heaven itself. It's a joy that reaches far beyond any earthbound joy and excitement.

"There is joy in the presence of the angels of God over one sinner who repents" (Luke 15:10). If the angels of God rejoice when a sinner is saved, surely the Lord who had compassion on the lost and the sick when He was on earth rejoices equally when disease-ridden or pain-filled bodies are set free by the power of the Holy Spirit.

But how do we get this spiritual power? How did John G. Lake get it?

Lake had no need for million dollar miracle services filled with pageantry and pomp, no need to stir up the audience with loud music and repetitious choruses, no need for a background organ to dramatize his voice when he talked. He needed only his hands and his voice and the power of the Holy Spirit flowing through him and out of him.

"In 1908, I preached at Pretoria, South Africa, when one night God came over my life is such power, in such streams of liquid glory and power, that it flowed consciously off my hands like streams of electricity. I would point my finger at a man and that stream would strike him. When a man interrupted the meeting, I pointed my finger at him and said, 'Sit down!' He fell as if struck and lay for three hours. When he became normal they asked him what happened, and he said, 'Something struck me that went straight through me. I thought I was shot.'

"At two o'clock in the morning I ministered to sixty-five sick [people] who were present, and the streams of God that were pouring into my hands were so powerful the people would fall as though they were hit. I was troubled because they fell with such violence. And the Spirit said, 'You do not need to put your hands on them. Keep your hands a distance away.' And when I held my hands a foot from their heads they would crumble and fall in a heap on the floor. They were healed almost everyone."

In his church in South Africa, Lake published a newsletter in 10,000 lots. It told about events that were taking place, such as salvations, deliverances, healings, and hundreds being filled with the Holy Spirit. When the newsletters were printed he had them sent to his tabernacle and would lay them out in packages of one or two hundred all around the front of the platform. At the evening service he would call the ones of the congregation that he knew to be in contact with the living God to come and kneel around and lay their hands on those packages of newsletters.

"We asked God that not only the reading material in the paper might be a blessing to the individual and that the message of Christ would come through the words printed on the paper, but we asked God also to make the very substance of the paper itself become filled with the Spirit of God, just like the handkerchiefs and aprons that came in contact with the apostle Paul's body became filled with the Spirit of God *(Acts 19:12)*."

Lake received thousands of letters from people telling how when they got the paper they were healed, or when they received the paper the joy of God came into their heart, or they received the paper and were saved by God. One woman wrote, "I received your paper. When I received it into my hands my body began to vibrate so I could hardly sit on the chair, and I did not understand it. I laid the paper down and after awhile I took the paper up again, and as soon as I had it in my hands I shook again. I laid the paper down and took it in my hands a third time, and presently the Spirit of God came upon me so powerfully that I was [filled with] the Holy Ghost."

Does that sound a bit far-fetched? Sound a little like something a televangelist would do today to get money? You're right, it does. But there is a vast difference — for John G. Lake and his Spirit-filled members it worked! And if it worked in their lives it can work in yours.

Surely there isn't a Christian today, from Pastor to church worker to church member, who would say that they are not interested in this kind of spiritual power. That they would not want it for themselves and for their church. That they would not want to see sick bodies and minds dramatically healed and addictions of every kind broken. That they would not want to see baptisms in the Holy Spirit with fire and power, and lost souls so powerfully brought into the kingdom of God that those newly-born cannot keep themselves from shouting and praising the living God and Christ our Lord.

So how can such spiritual power be obtained—how can *you* get it?

To learn that, we'll follow the journey of John G. Lake and learn how *he* got it. Having learned that, you can decide for yourself if you are willing to walk the same path, take the same journey, so that you also might obtain spiritual power.

Harold J. Chadwick

The Healer: Dr. John G. Lake

Biography by Ward M. Tanneberg, Ph.D.

Gordon Lindsay, co-founder of Christ for the Nations Institute, declared that in his opinion John G. Lake was "the greatest missionary that has appeared since the period of the Early Church."

John Graham Lake was born in St. Mary's, Ontario, Canada, on March 18, 1870. When yet a small boy, he accompanied his parents to the United States, settling in Sault Ste. Marie, Michigan.

In October 1891, he was admitted into the Methodist ministry in Chicago and appointed to the church in Pestigo, Wisconsin. He finally decided against going there and instead went into the newspaper business. In the Town of Harvey, Illinois, he founded the Harvey Citizen. (This town was named after D. L. Moody's brother-in-law.)

In February 1893, at age twenty-three, he married Miss Jennie Stevens of Newberry, Michigan. Three years later, she was pronounced incurable of consumption [pulmonary tuberculosis] by several physicians who had given her the best treatment then possible. They advised Dr. Lake to take her north. On that advice, Lake and Jennie returned to Sault Ste. Marie. Five years later on April 28, 1898, she received an instantaneous healing under the ministry of John Alexander Dowie. In Sault Ste. Marie, Lake opened a real estate office. As a salesman and contractor, he remained there until 1901. During this time, together with George A. Ferris, he founded the *Soo Times*, a local newspaper.

In 1904, he moved to Chicago and bought a seat on the Chicago Board of Trade with money borrowed from a friend. During this time, he handled Jim Hill's western Canadian land and made a long-time friend of this great railroad financier.

The first day he opened his office, he made $2,500 on a real estate deal. At the end of twenty-one months in the real estate business, he had over $100,000 in the bank, a $30,000 paid-up life insurance policy, and real estate valued at $90,000. He traveled to New York representing the Chicago Board of Trade. There he met Tom Lawson, together with Mr. Harriman and Mr. Ryan, all celebrated financiers. He was employed by Ryan to further his negotiations amounting to $170,000,000 in an effort to form a large insurance trust between the New York Life, Equitable, and Mutual Insurance companies. He also represented Mr. Lawson on the New York Board of Trade.

About that time, a huge scandal erupted in New York in relation to insurance companies. Mr. Lake, together with several others, organized the People's Life Insurance Company of Chicago. He was appointed manager of agencies and wrote a million dollars' worth of business in his first year. He had received a guarantee of $50,000 a year to continue in this business, but it was during this time that God dealt with him in such a way that the course of his life was definitely altered.

A number of years had passed since God had healed his wife, Jennie. During this time, he had continued practicing the ministry of healing. Every answer to prayer and miraculous touch of God created within him a greater longing for the deeper things of the Spirit.

During his business life, he made it a habit of speaking somewhere practically every night. After the services, he was in the habit of joining with friends who, like he, were determined to receive the baptism in the Holy Spirit as they believed the early disciples had received it (Acts 2:1-4). His prayer was, "God, if you will baptize me in the Holy Ghost and give me the power of God, nothing shall be permitted to stand between me and one hundred-fold obedience."

Sometime after this, he accompanied a minister to pray for an invalid lady who had suffered from inflammatory rheumatism for ten years. While the minister talked with the lady, John Lake sat at the opposite side of the room deeply moved in his spirit. He testified that he suddenly felt as though he had passed under a deep shower of warm tropical rain that fell not only upon him but through him. His whole being was soothed into a deep stillness and calm. An awe of the presence of God settled over him. After moments passed, he seemed to hear the Lord say, "I have heard your prayers, and I have seen your tears. You are now baptized in the Holy Spirit." Then Dr. Lake testified to "currents of power" that began to rush through his being increasing so greatly that his entire body began to vibrate intensely.

At this time, the minister friend asked him to join him in prayer for the woman. He found it difficult to walk across the room — the power of the Lord was so intense in his body. As he touched the sister's head with his hand in prayer, her clenched hands opened and joints began to work. The woman who had been an invalid so long arose from her wheelchair and was perfectly healed!

As a result of this baptism, Dr. Lake testified to seeing mankind through "new eyes." He had a great desire to proclaim the message of Christ and to demonstrate His power in the world.

In April 1907, he closed his office door for the last time and disposed of his bank account to various religious and educational institutions. Fred R. Burr of Winnemac, Indiana, who was his financial agent, assisted him in disposing of everything including his real estate holdings.

Dr. Lake started out in independent evangelistic work without a single dollar, being absolutely dependent upon the Lord along the faith lines of George Mueller of England and Hudson Taylor of the China Inland Mission.

During the next several months, he preached each day to large congregations with outstanding results. Many people received Christ as their Lord and Savior. Others were healed of diseases, while still others received the baptism in the Holy Spirit. While in a meeting in northern Illinois, the Lord spoke to him and directed him to go to Indianapolis to prepare for a winter campaign. He was instructed to acquire a large hall, and then was told that in the spring he would go to Africa.

Money Comes for Journey to South Africa

[One day during the following February my preaching partner, Tom Hazmelhalch, said to me, "John, how much will it cost to take our party to Johannesburg, South Africa?" I replied, "Two thousand dollars." He said, "If we are going to Africa in the spring, it is time you and I were praying for the money." I said, "I have been praying for the money ever since New Year's Day. I have not heard from the Lord or anyone else concerning it." He added, "Never mind, let's pray again."

A few days later he returned from the post office and threw out upon the table four $500 drafts saying, "John, there is the answer. Jesus has sent it. We are going to Africa."

We left Indianapolis on the first day of April 1908, my wife and I and seven children and four others. We had our tickets to Africa but no money for personal expenses en route except $1.50. But God continued to supply our needs throughout our journey.

Through my knowledge of the immigration laws of South Africa, I knew that before we would be permitted to land, I must show the immigration inspector that I was possessor of at least $125.00 We prayed earnestly over this matter, and about the time we reached the equator a rest came into my soul concerning it. I could pray no more.

About eight or ten days later, we arrived in Cape Town harbor, and our ship anchored. The immigration inspector came on board and the passengers lined up at the purser's office to present their money and receive their tickets to land. My wife asked, "What are you going to do?" I said, "I am going to line up with the rest. We have obeyed God thus far. It is now up to the Lord. If they send us back we cannot help it."

As I stood in line awaiting my turn, a fellow passenger touched me on the shoulder and indicated to me to step out of line, and come over to the ship's rail to speak with him. He asked some questions, and then drew from his pocket a traveler's checkbook, and handed me two money orders totaling $200.00. I stepped back into line, presented my orders to the inspector and received our tickets to land.]

Arival in South Africa

When they arrived at Johannesburg, South Africa, on May 15, 1908, Lake and his family had nowhere to go. They had no friends or acquaintances there. As they stepped ashore, a complete stranger, Mrs. C. L. Goodenough, walked up to Dr. Lake and said, "While in prayer last night, the Lord told me to meet this boat and said there would an American missionary on it with a family of nine, consisting of two adults and seven children and that I was to give them a home." At three o'clock that afternoon, the Lakes were living in a furnished cottage in Johannesburg that the Lord had provided for them.

Some time later [December 1908] at a native conference in the Orange Free State (Orange River Colony), Lake received a telegram from his oldest son, Allie, saying that his mother was ill and his father should come back immediately. Dr. Lake hurried back to Johannesburg but he was too late, Jennie died twelve hours before he arrived. She apparently succumbed to a heart attack brought on by a sudden onslaught of rheumatic fever. Prior to that, she had not been ill.

Early in 1909, Dr. Lake met Bishop Furze, the bishop of the Church of England for Africa. At the bishop's request, Dr. Lake arranged a series of meetings for the Church of England ministers. He was to teach them along the lines of divine healing. These meetings resulted in the establishment of the Emmanuel Society for the Practice of Divine Healing by the ministry of the Church of England in Africa. As word of these meetings and the work of the society continued to go forth, a committee from England came to examine and report upon Dr. Lake's work. He later accompanied that committee to England and conducted similar meetings in London under the direction of Bishop Ingram.

This conference authorized a committee to further visit other healing institutions in England and Europe. In the company of this committee, he visited healing institutions in London and went to Lourdes, France. There, they visited a Catholic institution where healing was reputed to take place by the waters of Lourdes and where they maintained a board of 200 physicians whose business it was to examine all candidates and report upon them.

At Lourdes, they were privileged to visit the then greatest hypnotic institution for healing in the world. This institution sent its representatives to demonstrate their methods to the Catholic board of 200 physicians, and hearing of the committee, they were invited to go along. Dr. Lake agreed to take part if he were given the final demonstration.

The committee selected five candidates who had been pronounced medically incurable. The hypnotists tried their various methods without success. Dr. Lake then had the five candidates placed in chairs in a row upon the platform in view of the audience of physicians and scientists. He prayed over each one of them separately. Three were instantly healed, a fourth recovered in a few days, and one passed away.

Dr. Lake returned to the United States for six months holding evangelistic crusades in Chicago, Portland, Oakland, and Los Angeles for the purpose of recruiting missionaries to take with him to South Africa. During these crusades, he acquired eight men but needed $3,000 for their expenses. While in Portland, praying alone in his room, he received assurance that the answer was on the way. Four days later in Los Angeles, a letter arrived at his hotel from George B. Studd of Los Angeles:

"My Dear Lake: There has been a windfall in your favor today. A person who does not wish to be known, gave me a draft of $3,000 saying, "God wants me to give this to Lake of South Africa." Am sending you, enclosed, therefore a draft for $3,005, the $5.00 being my personal contribution."

In January 1910, he returned to South Africa with his missionary party via London where he preached in Dr. F. B. Meyer's church and spoke in G. Campbell Morgan's weekly Bible classes—he did not speak in Campbell's church, however, because of a lack of time.

He returned to South Africa and remained there for several years during which time he founded the Apostolic Faith Mission with headquarters at Johannesburg. He was elected its president and continued for years after that to be its honorary president. During his ministry, he organized 125 white congregations and 500 native congregations.

Protection From Disease

In 1910, the African fever ravaged the area in which Lake lived, and in less than a month, one-quarter of the native and white populations died. Agencies of every description were called into action to combat the epidemic. Dr. Lake worked there with several assistants, four of whom died of the fever, but he never had a touch of the disease. He credited this to what he called the "law of life."

[Now watch the action of the law of life. Faith belongs to the law of life. Faith is the very opposite of fear. Faith has the opposite effect in spirit, and soul, and body. Faith causes the spirit of man to become confident. It causes the mind of man to become restful and positive. A positive mind repels disease. Consequently, the emanation of the Spirit destroys disease germs.

And because we were in contact with the Spirit of life, I and a little Dutch fellow with me went out and buried many of the people who had died from the bubonic plague. We went into the homes and carried them out, dug the graves, and put them in. Sometimes we would put three or four in one grave. We never took the disease.

During that great plague, they sent a government ship with supplies and a corps of doctors. One of the doctors sent for me and said, "What have you been using to protect yourself? Our corps has preventatives that we use as a protection, but we concluded that if a man could stay on the ground as you have and keep ministering to the sick and burying the dead, you must have a secret. What is it?"

I answered, "Brother, it's the law of the Spirit of life in Christ Jesus. I believe that if I keep my soul in contact with the living God, so that His Spirit is flowing into my soul and body, no germ will ever attach itself to me, for the Spirit of God will kill it."

He asked, "Don't you think you had better use our preventatives?"

I replied, "No, but, doctor, I think that you would like to experiment with me. If you will go over to one of these dead people and take the foam that comes out of their lungs after death, then put it under the microscope you will see masses of living germs. You will find they are alive until a reasonable time after a man is dead. You can fill my hand with them and I will keep it under the microscope, and instead of these germs remaining alive, they will die instantly." They tried it and found it was true.

They questioned, "What is that?"

I replied, "That's the law of the Spirit of life in Christ Jesus. When a man's spirit and body are filled with the blessed presence of God, it oozes out of the pores of your flesh and kills the germs."]

Due to the strain of overwork with the Apostolic Faith Mission, Lake ultimately gave up his ministry in South Africa in 1913 to return to the United States. There, he met and married Miss Florence Switzer of Milwaukee,

Wisconsin, on November 27, 1913. In addition to the seven children born from his first marriage, five more children were born into his second one.

Dr. and Mrs. Lake began traveling, stopping at Spokane where he was invited to open a healing room in that city. He accepted the invitation and ministered to the sick for about six months. Thus, he was to begin the ministry that really was the climax of his life's work.

The Healing Mission in Spokane

Dr. Lake's entire ministry had been profoundly affected by his exposure to John Alexander Dowie. Dr. Lake had been an elder in the Zion Apostolic Church when Dowie was at the height of his power. Thus he, together with various other persons exposed to the Dowie approach to Christian living, became dynamic disciples and missionaries of the gospel of Jesus Christ, coming west through the Dakotas, Montana, and into Washington.

Dr. Lake had made no preparation or study that prepared him for missionary work nor was he particularly trained in a theological perspective, as were most ministers. But he was a man of strong and forceful personality who seemed to make his way to the forefront in whatever situation he found himself.

His ministry had its weaknesses as well as its strengths. It was believed by some that his failure to properly anticipate the heavy responsibilities his first wife [Jennie] had to carry was an unfortunate mistake that contributed to her untimely death on the mission field. This fact, plus the responsibilities he now had in order to care for a large family, was one of the primary contributing factors to the close of his ministry on the mission field. However, his days of glory were not yet finished.

His early ministry in the City of Spokane became a demonstration of the power of God that resulted in more than 100,000 healings being reported during a period of five or six years. Some declared that Dr. Lake, through his ministry of divine healing, had made Spokane the healthiest city in the world. This, of course, was similar to a documented report that came out of Washington, D.C., some years earlier regarding Zion, Illinois, during the peak days of John Alexander Dowie's ministry.

His activity in Spokane had such impact that the *Spokesman Daily Review* carried full-page articles each week regarding his ministry and the miraculous acts of documented healing. The full-page articles in the Spokesman Review were often as follows:

The Church at Spokane

John G. Lake, Overseer

Divine Healing Rooms, 340 Rookery Building

Open each weekday from 10 to 4.

**Personal interviews and ministry
through prayer and laying on of hands.**

Public services on Sunday at

The Masonic Temple at 11 a.m. and 3 p.m.

Our ministry is private and confidential. Persons desiring to give public testimony must arrange with the ministers in advance.

Then would follow letters of testimony from those who had received healing or their physicians as well as articles by Dr. Lake.

In a general letter published Saturday, February 8, 1919, in the Spokesman Review, Dr. Lake indicated that they ministered to an average of 200 people per day in the healing rooms. He stated that over 60,000 personal "ministrations through prayer and laying on of hands" had taken place during the previous twelve months. In addition, calls for prayer and the ministry came by telephone, telegraph, letter, and cable from all parts of the world.

Ministry to the sick in their homes was another phase of work accomplished by the use of two motor cars in which ministers were conveyed from home to home, praying for those who were unable to present themselves at the healing rooms. Dr. Lake indicated that at least 100,000 people were ministered to each year by car, telephone, telegraph, letter, or cable.

Thousands of people would attend the Sunday services held each week at the Masonic Temple. Dr. Lake always liked to make a point of emphasizing that he did not spend money building church buildings and "sepulchers for the dead." Funds given to the church at Spokane would be used to send forth the gospel message into the world, according to Dr. Lake. There were no fees charged for any of the ministry, and the entire project was supported by means of love offerings. An especially appealing story was published on September 20, 1919, in the Spokesman Review. It was a testimony shared by Walter J. Williams, science department chairman of an eastern university.

In the article, he told about two of his friends in the East who had traveled to Spokane and received amazing healings. This scientist-educator was very adverse to anything savoring of what might be called the supernatural. But he journeyed to Spokane to gather first-hand information for himself. He visited several persons who professed to have been healed under Dr. Lake's ministry.

Then he visited the man himself. After an extended interview, he was invited to stay and see for himself what God was doing here.

Dr. Williams did.

> I saw them come, hundreds in a day. I talked to them, asking them questions, the lame, the poor, the rich, the uneducated, and the intellectual. Were they healed? Yes they were. Was I convinced that it was God? Indeed I was. The presence of God was there and I left Spokane inquiring if I was true enough to God to be trusted with His power as Mr. Lake and his associates were.

> I have listened to some of the greatest teachers on earth, both secular and religious, but I have never heard such revelations of life or such a revelation of God as I heard and witnessed at the Healing Rooms in the Rookery Building in Spokane.

Lake and Divine Healing Investigated

One summer, Dr. Lake and his staff were waited upon at their healing rooms by a committee of the Better Business Bureau of the City of Spokane. Their duty was to investigate the truthfulness of the public announcements that were continuing to appear in the city papers. For some time, Lake's staff had been publishing many of the testimonies of healing through the power of God that had taken place in the course of their ministry.

These testimonies were so astounding that complaints had reached the Better Business Bureau to the affect that the testimonies must certainly be untrue. The Better Business Bureau immediately undertook an investigation of the healing rooms' ministry and Dr. John G. Lake.

The committee examined eighteen witnesses whose testimonies had appeared in public print. Further names of persons who had received healings within the city were given to the committee so that they could go personally and investigate for themselves whether or not these things were so.

Dr. Lake suggested to the committee that on Sunday, June 23, at three o'clock in the afternoon in a public service, he would present 100 cases of healed persons for their investigation. He invited them to form a committee composed of physicians, lawyers, judges, educators, and businessmen who could render a verdict. During the intervening period between the interview in the healing rooms and Sunday, June 23, the committee continued their investigations.

On Friday, June 21, Dr. Lake received a letter from the committee assuring him that they had no desire in any way to interfere with the good being done and had determined that their appearance at the Sunday meeting would not be necessary. Two members of the investigating committee spoke privately to Dr. Lake and his staff and said that the committee was astounded. They had found out upon investigation that "the half had not been told."

One of the committee members visited at Davenport, Washington, and found printed announcements advertising a meeting Dr. Lake was about to conduct in the area. He inquired as to why these announcements were being made and the manager of the store replied:

"The whole countryside 'round Davenport is aflame with surprise at the marvelous healing of a girl in this community, well known to me, and, I believe, well known to yourself, Miss Louise Reinboldt, daughter of Mr. Jack Reinboldt.

"About three and a half years ago, Miss Reinboldt and her sister were operated on for what the doctors thought was appendicitis. The one girl died as a result of the operation. Louise came out of it unable to speak. She was taken to throat specialists, who pronounced her case absolutely incurable. Recently she was taken to Spokane to Mr. Lake's Healing Rooms and ministered to for twenty-six days.

"On the twenty-sixth day she startled her mother and family and, in fact, the whole countryside, by calling her mother on the long distance telephone and announcing to her in plain words the fact that she was healed. While preparing for her daily visit to the Healing Rooms, she had heard herself whistling and said, "Well, if I can whistle, I can speak also," and thus discovered that her paralyzed throat was fully healed."

After the Better Business Bureau committee backed away from further investigation, Dr. Lake announced that there would be no change in the program. He indicated the meeting would take place as announced, and if the Better Business Bureau would not take their place, he would appeal to the public for its verdict. Thousands of people attended that afternoon in the Masonic Temple while hundreds were refused admittance due to lack of space. Testimonies by ministers and lay people alike of significant, documented healings were given throughout the remainder of the afternoon. The publicity of this meeting was tremendous and was perhaps one of the high points in the sometimes controversial but always unique ministry of John G. Lake.

In May 1920, Dr. Lake moved to Portland, Oregon, to establish a similar work to that of his church in Spokane. Within a few years, this ministry in Portland was making a similar impact in Oregon as the one in Spokane had in Washington. One of his converts in Portland was Gordon Lindsay, who later became an independent Pentecostal evangelist of some significance and forerunner of the present Christ for the Nations Institute headquartered in Dallas, Texas.

Dr. Lake's ministry was unusual to say the least. He possessed a remarkable ability to create faith in the hearts of his hearers. Gordon Lindsay was no exception. Having followed Dr. Lake's ministry with deep respect and admiration, he one day had need of the great man's faith. He was stricken with a critical case of ptomaine poisoning and for days hung between life and death. Dr. Lake offered prayer for Lindsay, and although deliverance did not come immediately in a visible manner, he professed confidence that indeed the Lord had answered prayer. Mrs. Lake brought Reverend Lindsay some of the typewritten sermons her husband had recently given, and while reading these messages, faith suddenly sprang into his heart. He arose from what many thought was a deathbed, instantly healed.

While he was in Portland, Dr. Lake entertained hopes for raising up a chain of healing missions on the order of his works in Spokane and Portland. However, though he was not yet advanced in age, he had lived an intensity that had taken its toll. A decline in the strength and vitality that had characterized his earlier ministry became apparent. He seemed unable to match his spiritual vision with the physical strength required to bring it to pass. In Houston, Texas, he had some initial success in the founding of a church but was called away to the side of his eldest son who had suffered a serious accident that almost took his life. He never returned to Houston.

For a while, he ministered in churches throughout California. However, the dynamic touch that he once had was lacking. He later returned to the City of Portland where he pastored for a time. Afterwards, he returned to Spokane. There he pastored until his death.

On Labor Day, 1935, Dr. and Mrs. Lake attended a Sunday school picnic. He came home very tired and after a hot supper, laid down to rest. A guest speaker was at the church that evening so Mrs. Lake prevailed on him to stay at home. She went to church in his place. When she arrived home, she found that he had a stroke in her absence. He lingered for about two weeks, being unconscious most of the time, until September 16, 1935, when he went to be with his Lord.

His ministry was summed up in the brief testimony of Reverend B.S. Hebden who spoke at the memorial service.

Mr. Lake was a strong, rugged character of loving and winning personality, and he has left his mark indelibly upon the world of Gospel Truth.

Dr. Lake came to Spokane. He found us in sin. He found us in sickness. He found us in poverty of spirit. He found us in despair, but he revealed to us such a Christ, as we had never dreamed of knowing this side of heaven. We thought victory was over there, but Dr. Lake revealed to us that victory was here, a present and possible reality. We regarded death almost as a friend, but Dr. Lake came and revealed to us the Christ, all glorious and all powerful, that is triumphant, compassionate, and lovely, and our night was turned into day and despair was turned into laughter. A light shone in the darkness and we, who found Christ at last as He really is, only have words as the words of Thomas, who said, 'My Lord and My God.'

How I thank God that Brother Lake came to Spokane! How I thank Him that I ever contacted that man, unique, powerful! I will never forget the day in the Hutton Block when I was sick with several chronic complaints, and I heard that message of Christ, that His arms were under me, and I kept it and the message kept me and, instead of my being, long and long ago, gone and forgotten, I am here rejoicing and thanking our brother, Dr. Lake, who brought that message to me. Friends, he should still speak in me, not by the pen but by the Spirit that is in me, by the Light that is in me, by the regeneration of Jesus Christ that is in me. Let us, friends, not go and squander it by hiding it in a napkin, but let us keep it by giving it out.

Important Dates in the Life of John G. Lake

March 18, 1870 – John G. Lake is born at St Mary's, Ontario, Canada

1886 – Lake receives Christ as his Lord and Savior. His parents move their family to Sault Ste. Marie, Michigan.

1890 – Lake receives the experience of sanctification under the teaching of Melvin Pratt, a Christian farmer.

October 1891 – Lake becomes a Methodist minister in Chicago, Illinois. He doesn't pastor but starts two newspapers instead.

February 1893 – Lake marries Jennie Stevens of Newberry, Michigan.

1897 – Several physicians diagnose Jennie as having incurable tuberculosis – she also suffers from increasing heart problems.

April 1898 – Lake takes Jennie to the healing home of John Alexander Dowie in Zion City, Illinois, where on April 28 Dowie prays for her and she is instantly healed of tuberculosis and heart disease.

1901 – John and Jennie move their family from Sault Ste. Maria to Zion City, Illinois, where Lake joins the Dowie Institute.

1904 – Lake moves his family to Chicago and secures a seat on the Chicago Board of Trade.

April 1907 – Lake leaves his insurance business, gives away his wealth, and goes into evangelistic work, casting himself and his family upon God to supply all their needs.

April 19, 1908 – One year after beginning his evangelistic work, Lake and his family leave Indianapolis, Indiana, and head for South Africa to do missionary work.

May 1908 – John, Jennie, and their seven children arrive in South Africa.

December 24, 1908 – While Lake is attending a native conference in the Orange Free State, Jennie dies unexpectedly.

Early 1909 – Lake travels to England to hold meetings for Church of England ministers. As a result, the Church of England in Africa establishes the Emmanuel Society for the Practice of Divine Healing.

Early 1909 – From England Lake travels with a committee investigating healing to Lourdes, France, to visit institutions with a reputation for healing. The Investigative Council in Lourdes asks several there to attempt to heal five terminally ill people. Lake agrees on condition that he is the last to pray for them. All of the others fail in their attempts. Lake prays for the sick and three are instantly healed, one is healed over a few days, and one dies shortly after.

July 1909 – Lake returns to the United States for six months to hold evangelistic services. Sufficient funds are raised to enable him to take eight missionaries to South Africa.

January 1910 – Lake and his eight missionaries travel to South Africa.

1910 – Lake establishes the Apostolic Church and is elected president. Eight hundred Native Congregations and one hundred and twenty-five White Congregations are eventually organized.

1912 – Lake and his seven children return to the United States. He never goes back to Africa.

November 27, 1913 – Lake marries Florence Switzer of Milwaukee, Wisconsin. During their marriage, they have five children.

1914 – Lake establishes an Apostolic Church in Spokane, Washington, and opens Healing Rooms that draw thousands from the United States and other countries. Branch churches are established in Portland, Oregon; San Diego, California; and other cities.

May 1920 – John and Florence move to Portland, Oregon, to organize a similar church and healing rooms there. Within a few years, the healing rooms are having the same impact as the Spokane healing rooms.

December 1924 – During revival meetings at Lake's Portland church, Gordon Lindsay is powerfully converted. In 1970, Lindsay and his wife Freda co-found Christ for the Nations Institute in Dallas, Texas.

About 1925 to about 1930 – Lake attempts to establish healing rooms in Texas and various places in California but without success. He goes back to Portland to pastor for a short time and then returns to Spokane.

September 16, 1935 – At the age of 65, while pastoring in Spokane, Washington, John G. Lake dies of a stroke.

Photo Gallery

John G. Lake

1870–1935

John & Jennie Lake

John & Jennie with five of their seven children.
Back row: Jennie Stephens Lake, Alexdander, Horace Houghten (Joe),
John G. Lake.   Center: Otto Brian (Jack)
Front row: Irene (on Jennie's lap) and Edna, standing.
Not yet born: John Lake II and Wallace Stephens Lake.

John Alexander Dowie

Charles Parham

John G. Lake
Left and above: Probably about 45

Lake Evangelism Tent and Team

Ministry Team in Evangelism Tent

Portland Ministry Team Outside Church Building

John Lake and Florence, His Second Wife

Lake was among the early preachers at the Azusa Street Mission: William J. Seymour and John G. Lake seated, and Brother Adams, F.F. Bosworth, and Tom Hezmalhalch standing.

John Lake

John Lake — about 1934

John G. Lake — about 64

*Sacramento, California,
Mayor Welcoming Lake and Ministry Team*

ONE

Be Desperately Hungry

"Blessed are those who hunger and thirst for righteousness, For they shall be filled" (Matthew 5:6).

Desperation is like the pressure of boiling lava deep within the bowels of a volcano, held back only by the layers of inept material near the surface. But as the living lava continues to boil and seethe the pressure increases until nothing can hold it down and it breaks forth with a force that rolls over everything that tries to stop its progress.

Sometimes it's desperation for yourself, as it was for the woman with the issue of blood recorded in Matthew 9:20-22 and Luke 8:43-48, for Blind Bartimaeus recorded in Mark 10:46-52 and Luke 18:35-43, and for the Prodigal Son in Luke 15:11-32.

Woman with an Issue of Blood

Though the woman had an issue of blood and so under the law was unclean and forbidden to be in a crowd of people, her desperation, brought about by 12 years of unsuccessful medical treatment and having no money left to pay for more treatments, drove her through the law and the crowd of people to Jesus. She may have even forced her way through on her hands and knees, since the specific reference to her touching "the hem of His garment" may be there to indicate that she touched the bottom hem.

On her feet, on her hands and knees, forbidden by the law, scorned and discouraged by others, it did not matter. Her desperation was so great that whatever the cost she was going to reach her goal, "For she said to herself, 'If only I may touch His garment, I shall be made well.'" Everything and everybody get out of the way, a desperate woman is coming through!

Blind Bartimaeus

It was the same with Blind Bartimaeus. When he heard that Jesus of Nazareth was passing by, he cried out, "Son of David, have mercy on me!" Many of those there "warned him to be quiet." Be quiet. Be still. Don't make a fuss. Don't stir up things. You're disturbing everyone around you. Inept matter trying to hold back boiling lava that's bursting forth. Impossible!

So Blind Bartimaeus "cried out all the more, 'Son of David, have mercy on me!'"

When the Son of God heard this desperate cry, the Holy Scriptures tell us, "Jesus stood still." The timeless Christ stood still in time, captured by the cry of a desperate blind man who saw clearer than all those who would stop him.

Think of the wonder. The Son of God, by whom and through whom and for whom all things were created (Colossians 1:16), was arrested in His journey by the desperate cry of a blind person who sat begging daily on the side of the dusty and dirty Jericho Road. All because the blind person saw the truth of Christ the Healer!

So Jesus stood still and commanded him to be brought to Him. And when he had come near, He asked him, saying, "What do you want Me to do for

you?" He said, "Lord, that I may receive my sight"
(Luke 18:40-41).

You know what Jesus' answer was — the same as it will
be to you.

Prodigal Son

The prodigal son took everything his father gave him and
spent it upon the pleasures of the world until the world
took everything from him — as it does from everyone foolish
enough to do the same. To get enough food to stay alive he
was forced to take a job feeding pigs for no better food
than the pigs ate. An Israelite in covenant with Almighty
God through Abraham reduced by his own foolishness to
feeding animals declared unclean by the Law of Moses — a
spectacle to all who saw him.

Then he became desperately hungry, and that hunger
caused him to see himself as he truly was, to see his desperate
condition, and started him upon a journey home to his
father — a father of love and healing.

*"But when he came to himself, he said, 'How
many of my father's hired servants have bread
enough and to spare, and I perish with hunger!*

*'I will arise and go to my father, and will say to
him, "Father, I have sinned against heaven and
before you, and I am no longer worthy to be called
your son. Make me like one of your hired servants."'*

*"And he arose and came to his father. But when
he was still a great way off, his father saw him and
had compassion, and ran and fell on his neck and
kissed him" (Luke 15:17-20).*

Lake's Cry for Holiness

One night in Fred Bosworth's [F. F. Bosworth] home, before Fred thought of preaching the gospel, I listened to Lillian Thistleweight [sister-in-law of Charles Parham] tell of God and His love, His sanctifying grace and power, and what real holiness is. It wasn't her arguments of logic that impressed me — it was the woman herself. It was the divine holiness that came from her soul. It was the living Spirit of God that came out of her inner being.

I sat back in the room as far away as I could get. I was self-satisfied, doing well in the world, prosperous with all the accompaniments that go with successful life. But that night my heart became so hungry that I fell on my knees, and those who were present will tell you that they had never heard anybody pray as desperately as I prayed.

Fred said long afterward, "John, there is one instance that I shall always remember in your life. That was the night you prayed in my home until the rafters shook, until God came down, until the fire struck, until God came in and sanctified our hearts."

All the devils in the universe could not make me believe there isn't a real sanctifying experience of Jesus Christ. A moment when God comes in and makes your heart pure and takes self out of your nature, and gives you divine triumph over sin and self. "Blessed are those who hunger." Beloved, pray to get hungry.

As we talked with Lillian Thistleweight that night, I saw that the one supreme thing in that woman's soul was the consciousness of holiness. She said, "Brothers, that is what we prayed for. That is what the baptism brought to us. That is what we coveted from God."

Sometimes your desperate cry is not for yourself but for others, for those who are hurting, for those who are lost, for those who are sick and oppressed.

A Cry for Deliverance

I lived in a family, which for 32 years was never without an invalid in the home. Before I was 24 years of age, we had buried four brothers and four sisters, and four other members of the family were dying—hopeless, helpless invalids. I set up my own home, married a beautiful woman, and our first son was born. In only a short time I saw the same devilish train of sickness that had followed father's family had come into mine. My wife became an invalid; my son was a sickly child. Out of it all one thing developed in my nature: a cry for deliverance. My soul cried to God for deliverance. I knew nothing about the subject of healing; notwithstanding, I was a Methodist evangelist.

But my heart was crying for deliverance; my soul had come to the place where I had given up depending on man. My father had spent a fortune on the family to no avail, as if there were no stoppage to the train of hell. And let me tell you, there is no human stoppage, because the thing is settled deep in the nature of man — too deep for any material remedy to get at it. It takes the Almighty God and the Holy Spirit and the Lord Jesus Christ to get into the depth of man's nature, find the real difficulty that is there, and destroy it.

If you are away from God and your heart is longing, your soul is crying for God's deliverance, He will be on hand to deliver. You will not have to cry very long until you see that the mountains are being moved, and the angel of deliverance will be there.

I finally got to that place where my supreme heart-cry was for deliverance. Tears were shed for deliverance for three years before the healing of God came to us. I could hear the groans and cries, the wretchedness and sobs, and feel my family's desperation. My heart cried, my soul sobbed, my spirit wept tears. I wanted help. I did not know enough to call directly on God for it. Isn't it a strange thing that men do not have sense enough to call on God for physical difficulties, as well as for spiritual ones? But I did not.

Desperately Hungry

But one thing matured in my heart—a real hunger. And the hunger of a person's soul must be satisfied. It is a law of God that is in the depths of the Spirit. God will answer the heart that cries; God will answer the soul that asks. Christ Jesus comes to us with divine assurance and invites us when we are hungry to pray, to believe, to take from the Lord that which our soul covets and our heart yearns for.

One day the Lord of heaven came our way, and in a little while the cloud of darkness, that midnight of hell, was lifted. The light of God shone into our life and into our home. We learned the truth of Jesus as a present-day healer and were able to receive the divine power of God for our needs.

A History of Sickness and Death

No one can understand the tremendous hold that the revelation of Jesus as a present-day Healer took on my life, and what it meant to me, unless they fully understand my background.

I was one of sixteen children. Our parents were strong, vigorous, healthy people. My mother died at the age of seventy-five, and at the present time [March 1918] my father still lives and is seventy-seven.

Before my knowledge and experience of the Lord as our healer, we buried eight members of our family. A strange train of sickness followed us and for thirty-two years, there was always some member of the family who was an invalid. When I think back to when I was a boy and a young man I remember a nightmare of sickness, doctors, nurses, hospitals, hearses, funerals, graveyards and tombstones, a sorrowing household, a brokenhearted mother and grief-stricken father, struggling to forget the sorrows of the past, in order to assist the living members of the family, who needed their love and care.

At the time Christ was revealed to us as our healer, my brother, who had been an invalid for twenty-two years, and upon whom father had spent a fortune for medical assistance, was dying. He bled incessantly from his kidneys, and was only kept alive by eating as much blood-creating food as he could hold. I have never known any other man to suffer so extremely and so long as he did.

At the same time, my thirty-four-year-old sister was dying with five cancers in her left breast. Dr. Karstens, a German surgeon of good reputation, operated on her five times at Harper's Hospital in Detroit, Michigan. But it was no use. There was a large core cancer and after the operations four other heads developed—five in all.

Another sister lay dying of an issue of blood. Gradually, day by day, her lifeblood flowed away until she was in the very throes of death.

I had married and established my own home. Very soon after our marriage, the same train of sickness that had followed my father's family appeared in mine. My wife, Jennie, became an invalid from heart disease and tuberculosis. Her heart would stop and she would become unconsciousness. Sometimes I would find her unconscious on the floor or in her bed. Stronger and stronger stimulants became necessary in order to revive her heart action, until finally only nitroglycerin tablets would work. After these heart spells Jennie would remain in a semi-paralytic condition for weeks, the result of over-stimulation the physicians said.

Light Came Through One Godly and Courageous Minister

But in the midst of the deepest darkness, when baffled physicians stood back and acknowledged their inability to help, when the cloud of darkness and death was again hovering over my parent's family and mine, suddenly the light of God broke through into our soul through the message of one godly minister great enough and true enough to God to proclaim the whole truth of God.

I took my brother to one of John Alexander Dowie's great meetings in Chicago where a portion of the room was filled with cots on which dying folks lay. My brother, a man who had been an invalid for twenty-two years and the most terrible sufferer I have ever seen, was healed in that room. Dowie came in and sat down to teach for a little while and as he looked down and saw the intense suffering of my brother he dropped his Bible and came down to him and said, "Young fellow, I see you are suffering," and he prayed for him.

Instantly, the power of God flashed through him. He arose and walked out of the place in his nightgown. Three others, a great deal like him, were on cots. Dowie prayed for each one, and one after another received the healing touch and arose from their cots.

My brother walked four miles after he got off his death cot, returned to his home, and took a partnership in our father's business, a well man. When I saw him well, I walked on my tiptoes for about three weeks. The wonder of God's power had been revealed to my Methodist soul.

Great Joy and Hope

Great joy and marvelous hope sprang up in our hearts. A real manifestation of the healing power of God was before us. Quickly we arranged to take our sister with the five cancers to the same healing home, carrying her on a stretcher. She was taken into the healing meeting. Within her soul she said, "Others may be healed because they are good. I have not been a true Christian like others. They may be healed because of their goodness, but I fear healing is not for me." It seemed more than her soul could grasp.

After listening from her cot to the preaching and teaching of the Word of God on healing through Jesus Christ, hope sprang up in her soul. She was prayed for and hands laid on her. As the prayer of faith arose to God, the power of God descended upon her, thrilling her being. Her pain instantly vanished. The swelling disappeared gradually. The large core cancer turned black, and in a few days fell out. The smaller ones disappeared. The mutilated breast began to re-grow and became a perfect breast again.

Faith in Healing Springs to Life

How our hearts thrilled! Words cannot tell this story. A new faith sprang up within us — a living, dynamic faith. If God could heal our dying brother and our dying sister, and cause cancers to disappear, He could heal anything or anybody!

Sister Healed at Death's Door

The sister who had the issue of blood and I had been close from our childhood. She was a little older than I. The vision of Christ the Healer had just been opened to my soul. My mother called me one night and said, "John, if you want to see your sister alive, you must come at once."

When I arrived, my mother said, "You are too late, she is gone." I went to her bedside and laid my hand on her forehead; it was cold. I felt for a heartbeat but there was none. I picked up a small mirror and held it over her mouth, but there was no discoloration. She wasn't breathing. I stood there stunned. Her husband knelt at the foot of the bed weeping. Her baby was asleep in the crib at the opposite side of the room. My old father and mother knelt sobbing at the side of the bed. They had seen eight of their children die; she was apparently the ninth. My soul was in a storm. As I looked at this sister, I said, "O God, this is not your will. I cannot accept it! It is the work of the devil and darkness."

I discovered the strange fact that there are times when one's spirit lays hold on the spirit of another. Somehow, I just felt my spirit lay hold of the spirit of my sister. I prayed, "Dear Lord, she cannot go." I walked up and down the room for some time. My spirit was crying out for somebody with faith in God that I could call upon to help me.

That was twenty-five years ago when the individual who trusted God for healing was almost an insane person in the eyes of the Church and the world. Bless God, it is different now. That is the advantage of having people who trust God and walk out on God's lines to come together, stay together, and form a nucleus in society that has some force for God.

As I walked up and down in my sister's room, I could think of but one man who had faith on this line. That was John Alexander Dowie, six hundred miles away. I went to the phone, called Western Union, and told them I wanted to get a telegram through to Dr. Dowie with an answer back as quickly as possible. I sent this wire: "My sister has apparently died, but my spirit will not let her go. I believe if you will pray, God will heal her."

Soon after, I received this answer back: "Hold on to God. I am praying. She will live."

I have asked a thousand times, "What would it have meant if instead of that telegram of faith, I had received one from a weakling preacher who might have said, 'I am afraid you are on the wrong track,' or 'Brother you are excited,' or 'The days of miracles are past'?"

It was the strength of Dowie's faith that came over the wire that caused the lightning of my soul to begin to flash, and while I stood at the telephone and listened to his answer being read to me, the very lightning of God began to flash in my spirit. I prayed, "This thing is of hell; it cannot be; it will not be. In the name of Jesus Christ, I abolish this death and sickness, and she shall live."

As I finished praying, I turned my eyes toward the bed, and I saw my sister's eyelids blink. But I was so wrought up I said, "Maybe I am deceiving myself." So I stood a little while at the telephone, the lightning of God still flashing through my soul. Presently I observed her husband get up and tiptoe to the bed, and I knew that he had seen it.

I said, "What is it Peter?"

He replied, "I thought I saw her eyelids move." And just then, they moved again.

Five days later, my sister came to our father's home and sat down with us for Christmas dinner—the first time in my parents' life when all the Lake family was well.

The Healing of Lake's Invalid Wife

My wife, who had been slowly dying for years, and suffering untold agonies, was the last of the four to receive God's healing touch. But before God's power came upon her I realized, as I never had before, the character of consecration God was asking and that a Christian should give to God. Day by day, death silently stole over her, until the final hours had come. A brother minister was present. He stood by her bedside, then returning to me with tears in his eyes, said, "Come and walk."

We went outdoors into the darkness and he said to me, "Brother Lake, be reconciled to the will of God." Meaning by that as most all ministers do, "Be reconciled to let your wife die." I thought of my babies. I thought of her whom I loved as my own soul, and a flame burned in my heart. I felt as if God had been insulted by such a suggestion. Yet, I had many things to learn.

In the midst of my soul storm I returned to my home, picked up my Bible from the mantelpiece and threw it on the table. If ever God caused a man's Bible to open to a message that his soul needed, surely He did then for me. The book opened at the tenth chapter of Acts, and my eyes fell on the thirty-eighth verse, which read: "Jesus of Nazareth with the Holy Ghost and power: who went about doing good, and healing all that were oppressed of the devil; for God was with him."

Like a flash from the blue, these words pierced my heart. "Oppressed of the devil!"

Then God was not the author of sickness, and the people whom Jesus healed had not been made sick by God! Quickly going to another Scripture that was referenced, I read again from the words of Jesus in Luke 13:16, "Ought not this woman ... whom Satan has bound, lo, these eighteen years, be loosed from this bond?"

Once again, Jesus attributed sickness to the devil. What a faith sprang up in my heart, and what a flame of intelligence concerning the Word of God and the ministry of Jesus went over my soul. I saw as never before why Jesus healed the sick. He was doing the will of His Father, and in doing His Father's will, was destroying the works of the devil. (Hebrews 2:14b)

In my soul I said, "This work of the devil, this destruction of my wife's life, in the name of Jesus Christ shall cease, for Christ died and Himself took our infirmities and bore our sicknesses" (Matthew 8:16-17).

We decided on 9:30 a.m. as an hour when prayer should be offered for her recovery, and again I telephoned and telegraphed friends to join me in prayer at that hour. At 9:30, I knelt at her dying bed and called on the living God. The power of God came upon her, thrilling her from head to foot. Her paralysis was gone, her heart became normal, her cough ceased, her breathing was regular, her temperature was normal. The power of God was flowing through her person, seemingly like the blood flows through the veins.

As I was praying I heard a sound from her lips. Not the sound of weakness as formerly, but now a strong, clear, voice, and she cried out, "Praise God, I am healed!" With that, she caught the bed covers, threw them back from her, and in a moment was out on the floor—completely healed!

What a day! Shall I ever forget it—when the power of God thrilled our souls, and the joy of God possessed our hearts at her recovery?

The Truth Brings Healing to Thousands

"And you shall know the truth, and the truth shall make you free" (John 8:32).

The news spread throughout the city and the state. The newspapers discussed it. Our home became a center of inquiry. People traveled for great distances to see Jennie and to talk with her. She was flooded with letters of inquiry.

A great new light had dawned in our soul. Our church had diligently taught us that the days of miracles were past. Believing that, eight members of the family had been permitted to die. But now, with the light of truth flashing in our hearts, we saw that such teaching was a lie, no doubt invented by the devil, and diligently heralded as truth by the Church, thus robbing Christians of their rightful inheritance through the suffering of Jesus Christ. "… by whose stripes you were healed" (1 Peter 2:24b).

Others came to our home. They said, "Since God has healed you, surely He will heal us. Pray for us." We were forced into it. God answered, and many were healed.

Many years have passed since then, but no day has gone by in which God has not answered prayer. People have been healed, not by ones and twos, nor by hundreds, or even thousands, but by tens of thousands. For I have devoted my life, day and night, to this ministry.

Desperately Hungry

I wish we were all desperately hungry for God. Wouldn't it be glorious? It would be a strange thing if we were all desperately hungry for God and only one or two got filled [or healed] in a service.

"Blessed are those who hunger and thirst for righteousness, For they shall be filled" (Matthew 5:6).

Spiritual Principles

As with all principles established in the Word of God, the underlying principle stated in Matthew 5:6 holds true for anything that has been provided for us by Christ, whether righteousness, holiness, healing, spiritual power, or anything else. The underlying principle is this: Those who hunger and thirst, who are desperately hungry for what they desire, *shall* receive what they desire.

In spiritual matters, there is often a catalyst that explodes something within us and starts us on a new journey in the kingdom of God. For John G. Lake, it was when "the cloud of darkness and death" increasingly enveloped his beloved wife, Jennie, and threatened to blot out her life. So great was the darkness that all earthly hope was lost. But as in many things of the spirit, God used that darkness to bring forth the light of the truth of the healing gospel of Jesus Christ. It was a revelation that started Lake on a journey toward spiritual power unlike anything that had been seen since the time of the Apostles.

Beginning of the Azusa Street Revival

For Tom Seymour, the man God used to bring about the Azusa Street Revival[1] that swept the world, the spark that started him on his journey was the life of Charles Parham, whom God used to renew the spiritual gifts of the Holy Spirit to the Church.

> Brother Charles Parham was preaching in Texas. I was there when Tom Seymour came into his meeting. Parham related his experience with the Holy Spirit to Brother Tom and me. There was a deep hunger in Tom's soul. He worked as a waiter in a restaurant to support himself while he preached. He knew God as his Savior and Sanctifier. He knew the power of God to heal. But as he listened to Parham, he became convinced of a bigger thing—the baptism of the Holy Spirit. He went on to Los Angeles without receiving it, but he said he was determined to preach all of God he knew to the people, whether he had yet experienced it himself or not. Here is what he later told me.
>
> "Before I met Parham, there was such a hunger to have more of God in my heart that I prayed for five hours a day for two and a half years. I got to Los Angeles, and there the hunger was not less but more. I prayed, God, what can I do?
>
> "The Spirit said, Pray more. There are better things to be had in spiritual life, but they must be sought out with faith and prayer.

"I told Him that I was praying five hours a day now—but He didn't answer me. So I increased my hours of prayer to seven, and prayed on for a year and a half more. I prayed to God to give me what Parham preached, the real Holy Spirit and fire ... and love and power of God like the apostles had.

God had put such a hunger into that man's heart that when the fire of God came it glorified him. I do not believe any other man in modern times had a more wonderful deluge of God in his life than God gave to that dear fellow, and the glory and power of a real Holy Spirit revival swept the world.

That blessed man preached to my congregation of ten thousand people when the glory and power of God was upon his spirit, and men and women shook and trembled and cried to God. God was in him.

"Blessed are those who hunger ... for they shall be filled" (Matthew 5:6).

I wonder what you are hungering for. Have you a real divine hunger, something your soul is asking for? If you have, God will answer — God will answer. By every law of the Spirit that we know, the answer is due to come. It will come! Bless God, it will come. It will come in more ways than you ever dreamed of."

What will start you on your journey? What will God use to absolutely convince you of the truth of His Word, of the living presence of Christ the Healer in you, and that the same spiritual power that flowed in the life of John G. Lake is available to you? Watch for it. Be ready for it. It's coming.

My Own Testimony of a Desperate Cry

My wife, Beverlee, and I received Jesus Christ as our Lord and Savior in 1972. Within six months, the Lord began to progressively heal Beverlee of crippling rheumatoid arthritis and lupus. A few months later, He healed me of a slipped disk condition that for nearly ten years had periodically disabled my back.

Although our faith for healing had increased because of these, I continued to suffer from agonizing attacks of hemorrhoids—a condition that had recurred far too frequently for over 14 years.

The particular attack I'm writing about continued unceasingly for over two weeks, until I was apologizing almost daily to Beverlee and our children for my irritability. Going to work was impossible, as was a full night's sleep. I would awake almost every hour with nightmares of burning knives being plunged into me.

Toward the end of this two-week attack, nothing helped anymore to ease the pain—medication, hot baths, nothing worked. I prayed constantly for relief but without results. An operation was fast approaching as my only option.

This night of all nights, I used all the medication I could, took a hot bath, and then laid in bed on my back as quiet as I could. After some time I fell asleep—and then woke up about 1 A.M. with the most agonizing pain I had yet experienced. From my waist down I was literally on fire.

It was impossible to stay in bed, so I worked my way up and into the bathroom. There I grabbed the sink with both hands and braced my body against the waves of pain that roared though me. Sweat poured down my face as I stared at myself in the mirror, straining not to make a sound that would disturb Beverlee or our children. I had never before been in such agony.

I didn't know what to do anymore. I was desperate. I needed help. Then suddenly, in the midst of this agonizing pain, from somewhere deep inside, a cry burst out of me: "Jesus, help me!"

The pain instantly stopped, as if someone had taken a knife and sliced it away from me. It stopped so suddenly that my body, which had been braced against the pain, lurched forward and then back.

I didn't move a muscle. I hardly breathed. I just stood there, unable to believe what I was no longer feeling. I don't know how long I stood there, but at some point I moved slowly back into the bedroom and laid carefully down on my back and waited for the pain that I was certain would return – but which I hoped against hope would not. Then I drifted off to sleep.

When I awoke the sun was shining through our open bedroom window and I could hear birds singing in the backyard. Mentally I checked myself immediately for pain, and there was none, not a whisper, only a slight pressure where there had been agonizing pain for nearly two weeks.

Beverlee was still asleep and I got slowly out of bed and went over to the window and looked out at the backyard. A slight breeze was blowing, and the early morning sunlight was shining through the trees, chasing the shadows of the leaves on the lawn. I listened to the birds singing happily for the first time in two weeks—or so it seemed to me. Then suddenly I realized that the Lord had healed me and I wept like a baby.

That was thirty-one years ago, and there has never been another attack.

TWO

Be Fully Convinced

He did not waver at the promise of God through unbelief,
but was strengthened in faith, giving glory to God,
and being fully convinced that what He had promised
He was also able to perform (Romans 4:20-21).

At the end of a Sunday morning service in a nearby church, the pastor called several trustees to the front and announced to the congregation that starting that day they were going to lay hands on the sick and pray for them at the end of each morning service—to "see what will happen." Nothing happened, of course, and after several weeks the praying stopped without anything being said about it.

A few years ago a young lady from another church said that the intercessory prayer group in her church was praying and fasting for the pastor's wife to be healed of cancer. She was asked how often the group met for prayer.

"Every Friday night," she said.

"And how often is the group fasting?"

"All day Friday until after the prayer meeting."

"If your church's intercessory prayer group was absolutely certain that the pastor's wife would be healed if they prayed and fasted for, say, forty days, would they do it?"

"Of course," she said.

"And the intercessory group is not doing it because … ?"

If You Can Believe

Mark 9:23 records Jesus' answer to a father's agonizing cry for help after the Lord's disciples failed in their attempts to heal his son: "If you can believe, all things are possible to him who believes."

Think of it (Selah): "All things are possible to him who believes." Not just a *few* things, *all* things! No just *some* things, *all* things! Not just *most* things, *all* things! *Everything is possible to him who believes!*

Now here's the question: Do you fully, completely, absolutely, believe Jesus' statement that "all things are possible to *you* if *you* believe?"

You know, there are statements and promises in the Word of God that are so tremendous, so amazing, so immense in their implications that they stagger not only the mind and imagination but also the heart of many people — especially Christians. The statement or promise is just too great for them to believe. That's why the King James Version of the Bible puts Romans 4:20 the way it does: "He staggered not at the promise of God through unbelief … "

The KJV goes on to say in the next verse that he was "fully persuaded." The New King James Version that we're using for this book says that Abraham was "fully convinced that what He [God] had promised He was also able to perform."

Are you *fully convinced* that what Jesus said in Mark 9:23, 11:22-24, 16:17-18, and John 14:12-14 are true and He is able to perform them — perform them in your life and through you?

You must be, you know, otherwise you will never persist until you receive the spiritual power you need. Mark those two words well: *until* and *persist*. They are the two keys you need to unlock the doors to God's storehouse of spiritual power—or of anything else.

Insistent Persistence

In Luke 11:5-8, Jesus tells the story of a person who goes to a friend to get three loaves of bread for another friend (note that the loaves are for someone else). Though at first refused, he persists and is given what his other friend needs.

In verse 8, Jesus states that he is given the three loaves of bread specifically "because of his persistence." Then He gives the prayer principles and results of persistence in verses 9 and 10—most clearly shown in the Amplified Bible version:

And I say to you, Ask and keep on asking and, and it shall be given you; seek and keep on seeking, and you shall find; knock and keep on knocking, and the door shall be opened to you.

For every one who asks and keeps on asking receives, and he who seeks and keeps on seeking finds, and to him who knocks and keeps on knocking the door shall be opened.

Later in Luke 18:1-8, Jesus tells a similar story with the same prayer principles to His disciples to teach them "that men [you] always ought to pray and not lose heart."

It's worthy of note that in verse 5 where it says, "yet because this widow troubles me," it has the sense—as shown in the Amplified Bible—of, "continues to trouble me." Some say it's better interpreted as "continually continues to trouble me." In other words, the widow was insistent and persistent—she wasn't going to give up, to stop knocking at his door until he gave her what she wanted.

It is also extremely worthy of note that Jesus ended this parable of the insistent, persistent, widow with the question, "Nevertheless, when the Son of man comes will He really find [persistence in the] faith on the earth?"

Persistence *always* wins when you persist until! Persistence will overcome all obstacles, uncertainty, and enemies. It's the backbone of a conquering spirit that never retreats—the kind of spirit the apostles and John G. Lake had.

A Conquering Spirit

When we come down the line of twenty-one apostles, we find among other things that fourteen out of twenty-one gave their lives for the gospel of Jesus Christ. Five of them gave their lives on olive trees, where they did not take time to make crosses, but nailed them to the first thing that they could find. Thomas died in India being pierced through both ways and left to die. That is the character of apostleship; that is the character of Christianity.

That is the reason that before His arrest after He had eaten with them, Jesus took the cup and when He had drunk said: "The new testament in my blood." The thing that gave it significance was the pledge that was made. From time immemorial, men have pledged themselves under every circumstance. The old Romans, before a great battle were in the habit of gathering together, while the commander took the cup in his hands, to drink to the pledge that they all gave for the honor of Rome and that they would never retreat. That is what gave them their invincible character and that carried their conquest throughout the world.

Jesus Christ was not behind that conception in His endeavor to put that spirit of God and fidelity in the soul of Christianity. He called the twelve together, stood before them, and taking the cup in His hands said in their presence, "The new testament in my blood." And when He had drunk, He gave it to Peter and handed it to John, and to each one in his turn. And when they had drunk with the Son of God, accepting that pledge, it meant to Peter, "The new testament in my blood," and it meant the same to James and to Andrew. And to every one of them in their soul they gave assent to the pledge of Jesus, "The new testament in my blood."

That is the conquering spirit of apostleship in Jesus Christ, that conquering spirit of Christianity born out of the soul of the Son of God. That is the reason that Christians look to their Lord, not as a coward, not quailing from suffering and hiding in fear, but they look to Him as the boldest of the bold, as He dared to do what never man dared.

Who can help but love that character of a Christian? And beloved you who have listened to my voice for six or seven years past know that my heart has asked, my soul has cried, and my nature has longed that God might bring forth in this city [Spokane, Washington] a Christian character of that order that will stand forever as a divine monument of eternal faithfulness and fidelity in Jesus Christ to the truths of the Son of God.

Yes, I have confidence in you. Other souls may shatter on the rocks; other souls may wither in disappointment, but the lives that have been planted in that spirit of divine fidelity to Jesus Christ are unconquerable. They will triumph in the world. In the midst of the sentiment of modern church life, the world is waiting for those who dare again to walk out on the platform of the Son of God and stand there, bless God!

That is the reason that by the grace of God we take our place by the side of the Son of God and without dodging we endeavor to accept the platform on which our Lord has stood. "The Spirit of the Lord," said Jesus, "is upon me; because he hath anointed me to preach the gospel to the poor; he hath sent me to heal the brokenhearted, to preach deliverance to the captives, and recovering of sight to the blind, to set at liberty them that are bruised, to preach the acceptable year of the Lord."

Not the everlasting waiting for the year of the jubilee—no sir! Jesus Christ had come, the eternal jubilee, everlastingly available. He was at hand. Come in and take the blessing and by the grace of God enjoy the benediction of heaven that the Christ has provided.

My heart has ever coveted one thing above everything else; and that is that I might have been one of the company who sat with Jesus that night and might have taken the cup from His hands and drunk it like a man, saying, "The new testament in my blood." I bless God that throughout the ages, Jesus Christ has left a chosen church and a chosen generation of men and women who love the Lord, who can take the cup in their hands, and who can drink His blood again, declaring as He did, "The new testament in my blood," and live it and die by it!

Never Give Up—Never Retreat

John G. Lake would never give up or retreat before any disease or ailment or spiritual obstacle. Being fully convinced that Jesus Christ had provided redemption for the spirit, soul, and body of every human being who would believe, he wielded the name of Jesus Christ like the rod of Moses and drove back the enemies of God's children wherever he found them.

Blessed be God, if you were sick and the world was unable to help you, you would want a courageous, persistent, person with the conquering spirit of a John G. Lake to help you battle back your enemy. Lake had his

Alexander Dowie, and hundreds-of-thousands had their John G. Lake. Now the sick and diseased are waiting for others like them to rise up with the shield of faith, the sword of the Word, the name of Jesus Christ, and the power of the Holy Spirit.

Where are today's John G. Lakes, Alexander Dowies, Dorothea Trudels, A. B. Simpsons, A. J. Gordons, Maria Woodworth Etters, Smith Wigglesworths?

Look in your mirror!

Everything in Redemption is Available to Faith

Everything there is in the redemption of Jesus Christ is available for man, when man will present his claim in faith and take it. There is no question in the mind of God concerning the salvation of a sinner. No more is there concerning the healing of a sick one. It is in the atonement of Jesus Christ. His atonement was unto the uttermost, to the last need of man. The responsibility rests purely, solely, and entirely on man. Jesus put it there. Jesus said, "When ye pray, believe that ye receive them, and ye shall have them." And you shall have. No question about it in the words of Jesus.

If ever a man made his words emphatic, it was Jesus. If ever He spoke with emphasis on any question, it was on the subject of God's will, and the result of faith in prayer. Indeed, He did not even speak them in ordinary words, but in the custom of the East. He said, "Verily, verily." Amen. The same as if I would stand in an American court and say, "I swear to tell the truth, the whole truth, and nothing but the truth, so help me God." So the Easterner raised his hand and said, "Amen, amen," or "Verily, verily"—with the solemnity of an oath, I say unto you. So Jesus said, "When ye pray, believe that ye receive them, and ye shall have them."

James in expounding the subject says concerning those that doubt, "Let not that man think that he shall receive any thing of the Lord." Why? Well, he says a man that doubteth "is like a wave of the sea driven with the wind and tossed." There is no continuity in his prayer. There is no continuity in his faith. There is no continuity in his character. There is no fixed concentration on God for the thing that he wants. He is like the waves of the sea, scattered and shattered, driven here and there by the wind because there is an "if" in it. "Let not that man think that he shall receive anything of the Lord."

The redemption of Christ was an uttermost redemption, to the last need of the human heart—for body, soul, and spirit. He is a Christ and Savior, even unto the uttermost. Blessed be His Name! Who shall dare to raise a limit to the power of God! Who shall dare to raise a limit to the accomplishment of faith through Jesus Christ? I am glad that the days are passing quickly when men no longer desire to raise barriers before the souls of men. The tendency is to take down the barriers and let all the faith of your heart go out to God, for every man and every condition of life—to let the love of God flow out of your soul to every hungry soul.

Woman Healed of a Broken Back

People look in amazement in these days when God answers prayer for a soul. A week ago last night, my dear wife and I went to pray for a soul, a Mrs. McFarland. Ten years ago, a tree fell on her and broke her back. She became paralyzed, and for ten years she has been in a wheel chair, her limbs swollen, and her feet great senseless looking lumps that hung down useless. She says that many preachers have visited her in these years and have told her to be reconciled to the will of God, sit still, and suffer longer. She said, "Oh I would not mind waiting. If the pain would just stop for a little while, it would be so good. I would feel as if I were rewarded."

We lovingly laid our hands upon her and prayed. You ask, "Did you pray, 'If it be thy will'?" No! I did not, but I laid my hands on that dear soul and prayed, "You devil that has been tormenting this woman for ten years and causing the tears to flow, I rebuke you in the name of the Son of God. And by the authority of the Son of God I cast you out."

Something happened. Life began to flow into her being, and the pain left. In a little while she discovered that power coming back into her body. Then she found she could get up on her hands and knees. She began to call in her neighbors and relatives to show them what God had done and how God had delivered her.

Dorothea Trudel

About 1851 in Switzerland, God revealed to Dorothea Trudel that Jesus Christ was the same yesterday, today, and forever, and that all the healing power that was in Jesus was in Him still. That His love for humanity was still as deep as ever, and that He is just as willing to save a sick body as a sick soul.

Dorothea believed what she heard within her heart and read in the Bible and began to tell the glad tidings. Soon after, she healed several colleagues by way of prayer and anointing with oil. Others then began to come to her for prayer and anointing and many were healed. She later established the first divine healing homes using the same methods plus close attention to living a holy and righteous life. Along with the work of Bishop Blumhardt in Germany, this was the origin of the teaching of healing in modern times through faith in the name of Jesus Christ, and the forerunner of later healing homes and centers.

Faith Comes from Hearing
Dorothea Trudel Narrative

Charles G. Finney, during his lifetime, was familiar with the circumstances connected with the remarkable healing of a sick lady in Oberlin, Ohio, and he vouched for these facts as unquestionably authentic. This is what Finney said about the healing.

Mrs. Miller is the wife of a Congregational minister, and a lady of unquestionable truthfulness. Her story is worthy of entire confidence, as we have known her for years as a lame, suffering, invalid, and now see her in our midst in sound health.

Mrs. Miller and those who were present, regard the healing as supernatural, and a direct answer to prayer. The facts must speak for themselves. Why should not the sick be healed in answer to the prayer of faith? Unbelief can discredit them, but faith sees nothing incredible in the facts stated by Mrs. Miller. Mrs. Miller's own statement is as follows, and it is fully endorsed by the most reliable citizens and members of the First Church at Oberlin.

"From my parents I inherited a constitution subject to a chronic form of rheumatism. In early life, I was attacked with rheumatic weaknesses and pains, which affected my whole system.

"For nearly forty years I was subject to more or less suffering from this cause; sometimes unable to attend church services for months at a time. Until the last three months, I have been unable to get about without the aid of crutch or staff, generally both, for seven years. I have used many liniments and remedies, but with no permanently good result. I have been a Christian from childhood, but in our revival last Spring I received a spiritual refreshing from the Lord, which gave a new impulse to my faith. Since then, my religion has been a new life to me.

"Last summer, several of us Christian sisters were in the habit of spending short seasons of prayer together, that the Lord would send us a pastor. Some of our number had read the narrative of Dorothea Trudel, and had spoken to me on the subject of healing in answer to prayer.

"My faith had not yet risen to the level of healing. I had in fact accepted what I supposed to be the will of God, and made up my mind to be a lame and suffering invalid the rest of my life. I had long since ceased to use remedies for the restoration of my health. In fact, I had not even thought of praying in regard to it, for I regarded it as the will of God that I should suffer in silent submission.

"Notwithstanding what had been said to me about healing, I remained in this opinion and in this attitude until the 26th of September, 1872, when several ladies met at our house for a prayer meeting. I had been growing worse for some time, and was at that time unable to get out to attend a church service. I was suffering much pain that afternoon. Indeed, I was hardly able to be out of my bed. Up to this time, none of the sisters who had conversed with me about the subject of healing by faith had been able to tell me anything from their own experience, [they had only the information from Dorothea Trudel's narrative].

"That afternoon, one lady was present who could speak to me from her own experience of being healed in answer to the prayer of faith. She related several striking instances in which her prayers had been answered in the removal of different forms of disease to which she was subject.

"She also repeated a number of passages of Scripture, which clearly justified the expectation of being healed in answer to the prayer of faith. She also said that Jesus had shown her that He was just as ready to heal diseases now as He was when on earth—that such healing was expressly promised in Scripture, in answer to the prayer of faith, and that nowhere was it taken back.

"These facts, reasoning, and passages of Scripture, made a deep impression on my mind. For the first time I found myself able to believe that Jesus would heal me in answer to prayer. She asked me if I could join my faith with hers and ask for immediate healing. I told her I felt that I could. We then knelt and called upon the Lord. She offered a mighty prayer to God, and I followed.

"While she was leading in prayer, I felt a quickening in my whole being and my pain stopped. When we rose from prayer, I felt that a great change had come over me, and that I was cured. I found that I could walk without my staff or crutch or any assistance from any one. Since then, my pains have never returned. I have more than my youthful vigor. I walk with more ease and rapidity than I ever did in my life, and I have never felt so fresh and young as I now do at the age of fifty-two.

"The hundred and third Psalm is now my Psalm, and my youth is more than renewed, like the eagle's. I cannot express the constant joy of my heart for the wonderful healing of my soul and body. I feel as if it was every bit made whole."

The testimony of eyewitnesses to this healing is as follows: "We were all present at the time of the healing, and know the facts to be true. We are all Christians, and have no interest in deceiving anybody, and would by no means dishonor God by stating more than the exact truth.

"Since the healing, Mrs. Miller is still with us, and in excellent health. Neither the severe cold of last winter, nor the extreme heat of this summer, has at all injured her health. From our first acquaintance with her, she was so lame that she was unable to walk, except by the aid of crutches. Since that time she has been able to walk without help, and appears perfectly well."

Her husband added his testimony. "She was unable to walk without crutches for a number of years. A long time ago we tried many remedies and physicians, with no lasting good results, and expected that she would remain an invalid.

"Now she applies no remedy and has not taken any medicine. At the time of her cure she was much worse than for a long while before, being in great pain continually, until the moment she fully believed. When she did, she was restored to perfect soundness in an instant. From that moment to this, she has not felt any of her former pain.

"She can now walk with me for miles as fast as I want to walk without feeling much fatigue. She does all her own housework and attends seven church meetings during the week. In short, she is stronger, and seems as young and spry, as when we were married thirty-two years ago. The work of the dear Savior in her cure seems to be perfect, and she is an astonishment to all who knew her before and see her now. To His name all the praise.

"The same week my wife was healed, another lady who was a member of the First Congregational Church and confined to her bed with a complicated disease, was prayed for and restored at once to wholeness."

God is Too Great for Unbelief

It must be an insult to God for His children not to believe every word He says—an insult for them not to be fully convinced that He will do everything He has said and promised He would do. He is God, and He is too great for anyone not to believe Him fully—especially His children who are born again by His Spirit.

Jesus chastised His disciples for their lack of faith more than anything else. He got so exasperated with them that in Mark 9:19 He's recorded as saying to them, "O faithless generation, how long shall I be with you? How long shall I bear with you?" How long do I have to put up with your unbelief?

And when Peter failed to keep walking on the water because of his fear, even though most Bible versions have Jesus saying, "O you of little faith," the Greek New Testament shows that He actually called Peter "Little-faith." How would you like to have your Lord give you that name?

Don't doubt God; don't doubt His word. If you're going to doubt anything, doubt your doubts, they're unreliable. Be dedicated to God and single-minded — unwavering in your faith in Him, in the Holy Spirit, in Jesus Christ.

> *So then faith comes by hearing, and hearing by the word of God* (Romans 10:17).

> *Jesus said, "If you can believe, all things are possible to him who believes"* (Mark 9:23).

> *And Jesus rebuked the demon, and it came out of him; and the child was cured from that very hour. Then the disciples came to Jesus privately and said, "Why could we not cast it out?" So Jesus said to them, "Because of your unbelief; for assuredly, I say to you, if you have faith as a mustard seed, you will say to this mountain, 'Move from here to there,' and it will move; and nothing will be impossible for you"* (Matthew 17:18-20).

> *Jesus ... said to them, "Have faith in God. For assuredly, I say to you, whoever says to this mountain, 'Be removed and be cast into the sea,' and does not doubt in his heart, but believes that those things he says will be done, he will have whatever he says. Therefore I say to you, whatever things you ask when you pray, believe that you*

receive them, and you will have them" (Mark 11:22-24).

Most assuredly, I say to you, he who believes in Me, the works that I do he will do also; and greater works than these he will do, because I go to My Father. And whatever you ask in My name, that I will do, that the Father may be glorified in the Son. If you ask anything in My name, I will do it (John 14:12-14).

And these signs will follow those who believe in My name: they will cast out demons; ... they will lay hands on the sick, and they will recover (Mark 16:17-18).

THREE

Be Dedicated and Single-Minded

*I*n spiritual matters, there are three words that in any dictionary have similar meanings: *sanctify, dedicate, consecrate.*

Sanctify: To set apart for sacred use, consecrate.

Dedicate: To set apart for a deity or for religious purposes, consecrate.

Consecrate: To declare or set apart as sacred, to dedicate to a given goal or purpose (—adj. Consecrated to a sacred purpose, sanctified).

Many Christians, Dr. Lake among them, consider there to be a sanctifying sovereign act by God in which He purifies the heart of the individual and makes that person holy—usually based on 1 Thessalonians 5:23-24.

In this book, however, we are not using sanctify, dedicate, or consecrate to mean a sovereign act of God. We are using it to mean *you voluntarily and deliberately setting yourself aside for the purpose of being used by God to heal the sick and the oppressed.*

We have an example of this in Jesus Himself. In John 17:10, Jesus said, "And for their sakes I sanctify Myself, that they also may be sanctified by the truth."

Referring to this act of self-sanctifying by Jesus, the writer of Hebrews said, "By that will we have been sanctified through the offering of the body of Jesus Christ once for all." Meaning by this that as Christians we are set apart from the world for God's sacred use. But now as Christians, we must do as Jesus did and set ourselves apart—sanctify, dedicate, consecrate ourselves—to the sacred use, will, and purposes of God. For an example of this, see *John G. Lake's Consecration to God* at the end of this book.

Sanctify Yourself

To sanctify yourself means to set yourself apart for God's sacred use—to turn your heart from worldly desires and consecrate it to God for His cleansing and use. It is the direction of your heart that determines the direction you are going. As you think in your heart, so are you (Proverbs 23:7). Or to put it another way, you only do those things that you first see yourself doing.

Your body contains nearly 100 million receptors that enable you to see, hear, taste, touch, and smell physical reality. But your brain contains more than 10,000 billion synapses. In other words, God designed us so that we are 100,000 times better equipped to experience a world that doesn't exist—has no physical reality—than a world that does. A person, therefore, will rarely do anything that they haven't first seen themselves do in their mind—heart, if you will.

Why did God design us that way? So we will live, and can live, by faith and not by sight (2 Corinthians 5:7).

Jesus sanctified Himself, set Himself apart for the final work of the Cross. Someone once wrote of Him: "When it came time for His ascension, He set His face like flint toward Calvary." And that's what you must do to obtain spiritual power—set your heart and mind like flint toward your goal. Smith Wigglesworth said it another way: "Be in constant pursuit of all the power of God."

Like John G. Lake, set yourself apart for the task of having fulfilled in your life or ministry—and there should be no difference between the two—God's promise of the spiritual power needed to heal the sick and the oppressed of their mental, emotional, and physical problems. Cast aside all thoughts of personal glory, for God will not allow anyone to take the glory that belongs to His Son alone.

Like Jesus, sanctify yourself completely so that God can have a vessel dedicated to His purposes alone. Set your desires, your heart, fully upon this task. Don't have a divided heart or be double-mind.

> *... ask in faith, with no doubting, for he who doubts is like a wave of the sea driven and tossed by the wind. For let not that man suppose that he will receive anything from the Lord; he is a double-minded man, unstable in all his ways* (James 1:6-8).

Lake's Divided Heart

Shortly after my Baptism in the Holy Spirit, a working of the Spirit commenced in me that seemed to have for its purpose the revelation of the nature of Jesus Christ to me and in me. Through this tuition and remolding of the Spirit, a great tenderness for mankind was to awaken in my soul. I saw mankind through new eyes. They seemed to me as wandering sheep, having strayed far, in the midst of confusion, groping and wandering hither and thither. They had no definite aim and did not seem to understand what the difficulty was or how to return to God.

The desire to proclaim the message of Christ, and demonstrate His power to save and bless, grew in my soul until my life was swayed by this overwhelming passion.

However, my heart was divided. I could not follow successfully the ordinary pursuits of life and business. When a man came into my office, though I knew that twenty or thirty minutes of concentration on the business in hand would possibly net me thousands of dollars, I could not discuss business with him. By a new power of discernment, I could see his soul, understand his inner life and motives. I recognized him as one of the wandering sheep, and longed in an overwhelming desire to help him get to God for salvation and to find himself.

I determined to discuss the matter with the president of my company. I frankly told him the condition of soul in which I found myself and its cause. He kindly replied, "You have worked hard, Lake. You need a change. Take a vacation for three months, and if you want to preach, preach. But at the end of three months $50,000.00 a year will look like a lot of money to you, and you will have little desire to sacrifice it for the dreams of religious possibilities."

I thanked him, accepted an invitation to join a brother in evangelistic work, and left the office, never to return.

During the three months, I preached every day to large congregations, saw a multitude of people saved from their sins and healed of their diseases, and hundreds of them baptized in the Holy Ghost. At the end of three months, I said to God, "I am through forever with everything in life but the proclamation and demonstration of the Gospel of Jesus Christ."

I disposed of my estate and distributed my funds in a manner I believed to be in the best interests of the Kingdom of God, and made myself wholly dependent upon God for the support of myself and my family, and abandoned myself to the preaching of Jesus.

Will God Require the Same of You?

Will it be necessary for you to do what Lake did? Only God knows. God works differently with each of us. But God will give you the grace to do whatever He deems necessary for you to do to receive the spiritual power that you will need to do the work that He has already determined for you. It is always so, and His grace is *always* sufficient for the task (2 Corinthians 12:9).

Great spiritual power requires great dedication and separation. Not many, however, are willing to dedicate themselves and set themselves apart to obtain it, even when God clearly indicates to them that He will give them the spiritual power they seek if they will do so.

Kathryn Kuhlman often said that she knew that she was not God's first choice for the miracle ministry she had. She said that God had offered it to three men before He offered it to her, and that they had each refused it because the cost was too high.

How do you know if God is calling *you* to a ministry of spiritual power? Why are you reading this book? Curiosity or desire? If desire, recall that it is written, "Delight yourself also in the LORD, And He shall give you the desires of your heart." A wonderful promise, but most often misunderstood and misused.

Being spiritually logical, do you believe that God will give every desire that slides through a Christian's heart—taking into consideration the condition of most unsanctified hearts? Neither do I. But where do the desires of a sanctified heart come from—the desires of those who "delight themselves in the LORD"? From the LORD Himself, of course. And He will *always* give you the desires that He puts into your heart! That's why He gave John G. Lake the spiritual power he needed to do what God had already determined he should do. And that's why He will give *you* similar spiritual power.

For Everything Worthwhile There is a Cost

I know a minister who often prayed for spiritual power, and time-and-again when he prayed, he was asked these questions by the Lord, "How badly do you want it? Are you willing to do whatever it costs to get it?"

For everything in life that is worthwhile, there is a cost, a price that must be paid. This is especially true in spiritual matters. For spiritual power, each individual must pay the price. There are no exceptions. There are no cloned Christians.

Though material wealth may be inherited, passed from one to another, this is not true of spiritual power, no matter how many claim to the contrary that they have received the so-called *anointing* of another. What is true in spiritual matters is what David du Plessis (Mr. Pentecost) told a man on an airplane about the necessity of each person being born-again: "God has no grandchildren."

God Will Not Give
Spiritual Power to the Unsanctified

God will not give true spiritual power, as contrasted to what purports to be spiritual power, to those who do not set themselves apart, sanctify themselves as Jesus did, for His sacred use—and for control by the Holy Spirit when He so deems it necessary. It is God's power and must always remain under His control. He never imparts it to anyone to use for his or her own selfish purposes, to use in ways outside of His will, or to use in ways that brings glory to the individual and not to Jesus Christ.

Anything that falls outside of those three categories is pseudo-power and not real spiritual power. It is not from God, but is power that is of man or another source; a source that may even deceive the individual, and those who gather to wonder and marvel, into believing it is the power of the Holy Spirit.

Keep Yourself from Being Deceived

How will *you* keep yourself from being deceived by pseudo-power, false power that is not of God as you pursue your goal of true spiritual power? By one of the spiritual principles that God has established: sanctify yourself, set yourself aside for God's sacred use, and let Him cleanse your heart so you will clearly hear His voice. Dr. Lake tells about a man in Africa who did just that and what resulted from it.

Miracle Ministry of William T. Dugan

One Sunday afternoon a tall Englishman walked into my church in Johannesburg, South Africa. He had a top of red hair that made him as conspicuous as a lion. He walked up the aisle and took a seat quite near the front. My old preaching partner was endeavoring to explain the mighty power of the living Christ as best he could, and this man sat listening. Presently he arose, saying, "Sir, if the things you are talking about are all right, I am your candidate."

He added, "I used to be a Christian, but I came to Africa and lived the usual African life and the result is that for three years I have been unable to do anything and my physicians say I am incurable. Tell me what to do!"

My old partner asked, "John, what shall we do?" I replied, "Call him up; we shall pray for him right now."

We stepped off the platform, put our hands on William T. Dugan, and instantly—as a flash of lightning blasting a tree or rock—the power of God went through the man's being, and the Lord Jesus Christ made him well.

A few days afterward he came to my house in the middle of the day and said, "Lake, I want you to show me how to get a clean heart." I took the Word of God and went through it with him to show him the mighty, cleansing, sanctifying power of the living God in a man's heart. Before he left, he knelt by a chair and consecrated his life to God.

Three months passed. One day he called and said, "I have a call from God." I knew it was. There was no mistaking it. The wonder of it was in his soul. He went down into the country where a great epidemic of fever raged. Some weeks afterward I began to receive word that people were being healed. Hundreds of them! Thousands of them! One day I concluded I would go down and join in the same work a couple of hundred miles from where he was. Somehow, the news traveled to him where I was, and he came there.

The next afternoon we called at the home of a man who said his wife was sick with diabetes. We prayed for the wife and several other persons who were present. Then a man stepped out into the kitchen and asked, "Would you pray for a woman like this?" When I looked at her, I saw she had clubfeet. The right foot was on an angle of 45 degrees and the left at right angles.

Dugan replied, "Yes. Pray for anybody." He said to her, "Sit down," and taking the clubfoot in his hands he said, "In the name of Jesus Christ become natural." And I want to tell you that man is in the glory presence of God today and I am going to stand there with him some day. Before I had a chance to take a second breath, that foot commenced to move, and the next instant that foot was straight!

Then he took up the other foot saying, "In the name of Jesus Christ become natural." Beloved, it was not the voice of the man, nor the confidence of his soul, but the mighty divine life of Jesus Christ that flashed through him and melted that foot into softness and caused it instantly to become normal by the power of God.

10,000 People Healed in 16 Months

We have not even begun to touch the fringes of the knowledge of the power of God. However, I want to encourage your hearts. I am glad we can say what perhaps has never been said in the Christian world from the days of the apostles to the present time, that since the opening of this work in Spokane, about sixteen months ago, ten thousand people have been healed by the power of God. (Written about 1916.)

Jesus' Prayer for His Disciples and Us

In His high-priestly prayer to His Father in John 17, Jesus said, "Sanctify them by Your truth. Your word is truth ... And for their sakes I sanctify Myself, that they also may be sanctified by the truth" (John 17:17, 19).

Therefore, like Jesus did—and like John G. Lake, Smith Wigglesworth, Kathryn Kuhlman, Charles Price, William T. Duggan, and countless others did throughout the grand history of the Church—sanctify yourself for the sake of the oppressed, the sick, and the lost so that you may set them free and heal them in the name of Jesus Christ.

Dr. Lake brought deliverance, healing, and salvation to hundreds-of-thousands. It is said that in a five-year period in Spokane, Washington, Lake and his staff recorded healings of over 100,000 people. So many that Spokane was declared to be the healthiest city in the United States. Many of the physical afflictions were of such a nature that nothing could have healed them except the true spiritual power of God—the kind of power you want.

Healing Testimonies at a Public Meeting

Spokane, Washington, Summer of 1918 or 1919

Malignant Tumor

Reverend R. Armstrong, a Methodist minister, of N2819 Columbus Avenue, healed of a sarcoma growing out of the left shoulder three times as large as a man's head, was healed in answer to prayer.

Breast Cancer

Mrs. Chittenden, pastor of the Church of the Truth at Coeur d'Alene, Idaho, testified to her healing of cancers of the breast; one breast having been removed in an operation and the other breast becoming likewise affected with cancer. She was healed of the Lord in answer to prayer.

Varicose Veins

Mrs. Everetts, 1911 Boone Avenue, testified to her healing of varicose veins. She had suffered from them for thirty-eight years. The veins were enlarged until they were the size of goose eggs in spots. Under the right knee, there was a sack of blood so large that the knee was made stiff She had exhausted every medical method. After being ministered to at the Healing Rooms for a short period,* she was entirely well and the veins are perfectly clear.

[*Lake and his healing technicians always prayed for the person until they were healed, whether the person was healed instantly or it took hours, days, weeks, or months of repeated ministering and praying.]

Internal Cancer and Neuritis

Mrs. Walker, Granby Court, was an invalid at the Deaconess hospital from internal cancer; after an exploratory operation, the disease was pronounced incurable by the doctors. She also had a severe case of neuritis. Her suffering was unspeakable. She testified to her healing and of her restoration to perfect health, the cancer having passed from her body in seven sections. Since then, many have been healed through her prayer and faith.

Inflammatory Rheumatism

Mrs. O. D. Stutsman, Hansen Apartments, testified to having been an invalid for thirteen years. On one occasion, she lay in the Sacred Heart Hospital with a twenty-pound weight attached to her foot for thirty-two days, while suffering from inflammatory rheumatism. Her suffering was so intense that she begged her husband to take her home, preferring to remain a cripple rather than endure such suffering. The Reverend Lake was called to minister to her at her home; as prayer was offered, the power of the Spirit of God surged through her. Five minutes after his hands were laid upon her she arose from her bed, perfectly healed.

Fibroid Tumors and Restoration of Organs

Mrs. John A. Graham, E369 Hartson, a nurse and hospital matron, was operated on for fibroid tumors. The generative organs were removed and at a later date, she was operated on a second time for gallstones. The operation not being a success, she was eventually left to die, and when in the throes of death and unconscious, she was healed by the power of God in answer to prayer of one of the ministers called from the healing Rooms. The organs that had been removed in the operation regrew in the body, and she became a normal woman and a mother.

Dislocated Hip Healed from a Distance

Mrs. O. Gilbertson, N4115 Helena Street, testified that through disease, her hip came out of joint and her limb would turn like the leg of a doll, showing that it was entirely out of the socket. Her home is about five miles distant from the Healing Rooms. Reverend Lake and his co-workers engaged in prayer for her at the Healing Rooms, and as prayer was offered the power of God came upon her [at home], resetting the joint.

The following remarks were made by the Reverend Lake as the testimony was given:

"Do you hear it, you folks who worship a dead Christ? You doctors hear it? You preachers who lie to the people and say the days of miracles are past, do you hear it? You doubters hear it? God set the woman's hip. Because faith in God applied the blessed power of God to her life and limb."

Dedicated and Single-minded

To be dedicated and single-minded in your pursuit of the kind of spiritual power that John G. Lake had, you must be a constant consumer of the meat of the Word of God. The Holy Spirit can only use the amount of the Word that is in you. He will teach you the deep things of the Scriptures as you meditate upon them, and will remind you of what He has taught you and teach you even more at the times you need them. So be filled with the Word of God.

FOUR

Be Filled with the Word of God

It is the Spirit who gives life; the flesh profits nothing. The words that I speak to you are spirit, and they are life (John 6:63).

So then faith comes by hearing, and hearing by the word of God (Romans 10:17).

Almost without exception, every person great for God has been a person of the Word of God—a person who loved and lived the Word. And almost without exception, the decline of every person great for God can be directly traced to a decline in their love and study of the Word of God. Rather than continuing to feed daily upon the fresh bread of the Word of God, they tried to maintain their spiritual strength with what they had eaten in days and years past. And gradually the ways of the Word slipped away from them and were replaced with the ways of the world.

An Evil Heart of Unbelief

The book of Exodus tells us that the Israelites did not have the faith to go into the Promised Land and drive out the enemies of God who were squatters on the land He had promised to Abraham. Hebrews 3:19 says, "They could not enter because of unbelief," and warns us all in verse 3:12, "Beware, brethren, lest there be in any of you an evil heart of unbelief in departing from the living God."

Because of their unbelief—their total lack of faith in the power of God—Psalm 78:40 says, " ... again and again they tempted God, And limited the Holy One of Israel." Think of that—their unbelief limited God. He could not do what He wanted to do for them, and through them, because they would not believe Him and obey Him. Verse 78:42 says, "They did not remember His power."

How often in our lives has our unbelief limited God? How often has it prevented Him from doing what He wanted to do for us or through us because we did not have the faith in Him to move forward when He was urging us to do so?

If you want to minister to the sick and oppressed, to set them free and heal them, then for their sakes, and for the sake of the glory of God and Jesus Christ, you cannot— must not—limit God by your unbelief.

How do you get rid of unbelief?

The Scriptures say this about the Old Covenant Israelites:

> *Now all these things happened to them as examples, and they were written for our admonition, upon whom the ends of the ages have come.* (1 Corinthians 10:11)

So we of the New Covenant are supposed to learn from their bad examples the right things we should do in relation to God and Christ. In other words, don't do what they did and suffer the same kind of consequences. Do what God tells us to do and receive the results and blessings He promises us.

Every Word of God

When the Israelites would not obey God because of their unbelief and go into the Promised Land, God turned them back into the wilderness to wander for forty years until all of the adult generation had died. During those forty years, He fed them only manna.

Now it is important to us that we realize that our omnipotent God could have fed them with the finest food of the earth—if He had wanted to. Or He could have fed them with a great variety of heavenly food finer than all the finest food of the earth—if He had wanted to. But He fed them *only* manna—a sweet, wafer-like, food that appeared on the ground each morning except on the Sabbath.

Now there are those of the prosperity persuasion who have used the manna to develop doctrines about God's abundant provisions for you when things are going bad. But the manna had nothing to do with that. Think of it: forty years of raw manna, boiled manna, fried manna, manna-a-manna, manna sandwiches (manna between two manna wafers)—manna for breakfast, manna for lunch, manna for dinner, and manna snacks in-between. Nothing but manna and more manna for forty years! And all when God was fully capable of providing the Israelites with the finest and tastiest of foods—if He had wanted to.

So why did He feed them nothing but manna for forty years? God, of course, does nothing without a reason and a purpose—and Moses tells us what those were in Deuteronomy 8:1-3.

> *Every commandment which I command you today you must be careful to observe, that you may live and multiply, and go in and possess the land of which the LORD swore to your fathers.*

> *And you shall remember that the LORD your
> God led you all the way these forty years in the
> wilderness, to humble you and test you, to know
> what was in your heart, whether you would keep
> His commandments or not.*

> *So He humbled you, allowed you to hunger, and
> fed you with manna which you did not know nor
> did your fathers know, that He might make you
> know that man shall not live by bread alone; but
> man lives by every word that proceeds from the
> mouth of the LORD.*

God could not have the next generation of Israelites
disobey Him also because of unbelief and refuse to go into
the Promised Land. It wasn't only His promise to Abraham
that must be kept. The land of Canaan was essential to His
eternal purpose in Christ, and for that purpose to be fulfilled
the land must be possessed by His people—for where God's
people are and walk in obedience, God is there as God of
the land. He is everywhere, of course, but His presence is
manifested only where He has obedient people. It is a
principle throughout the Bible that whenever God wants
to do something in a particular place, He always sends His
people there and does it through them—that is, through
the ones who are obedient to Him. Think of Moses being
sent to Egypt, Jesus being sent to the earth, John G. Lake
being sent to Africa.

So to rid the Israelites of any unbelief that might make
them disobey Him, God humbled them and put them on a
forty-year fast of manna so that they would learn that His
children are not to live by physical food alone, but by *every*
word that comes forth from the mouth of God.

You will recall that hundreds of years later, at the end
of a forty-day fast put upon Him by the Holy Spirit, Jesus

quoted the spiritual principle from Deuteronomy 8:3 to the devil when he tried to tempt Him to turn stones into bread. And a few years later, He used the other spiritual principle that God had established and told His disciples that they could not cast a demon out of a little boy because of their unbelief. That a spirit of infirmity that had been in someone for a long time could only come out through prayer and fasting. (Matthew 17:14-21, Mark 9:14-29).

Putting those two principles together, it is easy for us to realize that God has given us His Word, fasting, and prayer to enable us to rid ourselves of unbelief and give greater force to our faith.

Just as we physically live and grow by the food of the earth that God has given us, we must spiritually live and grow by the food of heaven that God has given us. There is no other way to physically live and grow, and there is no other way to spiritually live and grow. If we refuse or neglect to eat physical food, we physically die, and if we refuse or neglect to eat spiritual food, we spiritually die. To try to spiritually live and grow without the spiritual food God has given us makes as much sense as trying to live and grow without the physical food God has given us. Neither is possible. It's as simple and direct as that. Here is what John G. Lake has to say about it.

Now let me state it again: You may be a great spiritual athlete: you may have been a great spiritual athlete, but somewhere you've stopped feeding on the Word. The Word lost its flavor and taste to you.

I know of preacher after preacher who had great power at one time, but they have lost all the joy in the Scripture. How do I know? Well, I know by the way they act. When a man loves a woman, he wants her to be with him, doesn't he? He doesn't care to go off and spend evenings alone. And when a man loves his Bible, you will find the Bible with him, in his arms, somewhere. He has gotten hold of the thing. He is holding it.

When I find a man along in years, his hair is growing gray, and I see that he loves the Bible, I know that man is fresh in his spirit life.

You can trace the downfall of every spiritual giant that I have ever known in my life to one of these three things.

The First Thing

He's lost his desire for the Book. I heard one of the greatest men this country ever produced, when that Book was in his hand, when he preached just like this. He drove me to my knees. Every time I would hear him I would go out, get alone, and pray if I could possibly do it. He filled me, thrilled me, and lifted me. I saw him 20 years later when his name was on the lips of every man. I heard him preach, and I noticed that he quoted a good many Scriptures, but he never picked up his Bible. I noticed he had a theory and a philosophy of redemption instead of the old-time simple exposition of the Word. And I saw that man whose name was known in every part of the world with something like 60 churches sponsoring him in a building that seated about 3500, and the building was not half full. He had the greatest Gospel soloist that this country had ever produced, but the meeting was as dry and dead as any formal service imaginable. I said to the singer who left that field and came with me for a campaign or two, "Charlie, what is the matter with him?"

"Well," he replied, "I don't know, but he is no more like the man he used to be than anything in this world."

There had been no sin come into that man's life—his life was just as clean as it had ever been. But here is how it had come: somehow or other he had broken in his spiritual life with the food of the Spirit—the Bible. And the second thing, he used to have the most marvelous prayer life—he didn't have it any more. And the third thing in that whole sermon I didn't hear one personal confession, because he was preaching in a place where personal confession was taboo. People criticized it. If you said anything about yourself and your own experience, the ministers right off the first thing would say, "He is bragging about his own life, isn't he?"

Brothers and sisters, you will brag about your own life if you have power with God, and you can't help this bragging; you have something to brag about. You have a walk in the fullness of the life and fellowship of your spirit with His spirit, and you have something to talk about, haven't you? Fresh new experiences are coming into you all the time. You are walking in the realm of miracles. I knew that man when he walked in the creative realm of faith. I knew him later when he moved down into the purely intellectual realm.

Physical Healing is Spiritual

Healing is basically a spiritual thing. The power that heals the sick comes from God down through your spirit, out through your hands into that man or woman. If you are having the right kind of spiritual fellowship, you will have power with God, and there is no escaping it. But listen, brothers and sisters, you can't get a powerful current of divine life from a little impoverished wire, can you? And you can't get it when the wire where it connects with you is corroded with worldly cares.

You say, "I will tell you what I want. I want to be able to stand about 10,000 volts. I want to be wired up to God so that the fullness of His power can pour down through me, through my soul, out through my hands and voice to the people."

It doesn't take much to break the connection of your spirit and His. God is a spirit. You are a spirit. Something breaks the connection, and the power no longer flows through. You ask me to pray for you. There is no power. What is the matter? Something has broken the connection. The power comes through the one who prays, but it can't get through your spirit and touch you.

But suppose you and I are both right in our spirits. You will get your healing as sure as God sits on His throne. "But if the Spirit of him that raised up Jesus from the dead dwell in you, he that raised up Christ from the dead" shall send healing through your spirit and into your mortal flesh.

The Second Thing

What must be done continually is that after you have fed on the Word, you must open your spirit to confession. You can't bottle up God. He will use you to communicate to others. You act as a medium to communicate Him to others by message or testimony or prayer. You are His instrument through which He is going to work. Beautiful, isn't it?

The Third Thing

Now you see that keeps you in perfect communion because you have to get new messages continually from Him, so you live in perfect fellowship with Him, feeding on His Word and telling of the things He does for you. And no Christian can long survive that does not have a present tense up-to-date testimony. No Christian is safe that hasn't a now experience with the Lord because sickness can come on you and you have no power to throw it off [or to drive it away from others].

Three things. One, feeding on the Word. Two, a continual public confession of what you are and what Jesus Christ is to you. I'm not talking of sin. I mean confession of your faith in Christ, of what Christ is to you—of His fullness, of His completeness, and of His redemption. Three, communion with Him. Feeding on the Word, confession, and communion. Three simple things, aren't they? Yet, they are the things that produce great spiritual life. You do not have it without them.

The Word of God, prayer, and testifying to the things that God has done for you will build your spiritual strength and keep you strong.

The Creative Word

The following is from a small book written by Dr. Charles S. Price titled *The Creative Word*.

"It is the Spirit who gives life; the flesh profits nothing. The words that I speak to you are spirit, and they are life" (John 6:63).

The Bible is not a textbook. It is true that it records history and is replete with fascinating narrative, but to accept it as an instruction book regarding life or a guide book to tell us about the way home is to miss its meaning and its power.

The Egyptians have a book called *The Book of the Dead.* As a matter of fact, all ethnic writings can be described as dead for they tell only of dead souls and dead creeds and dead philosophies and dead empires. They can be summarized as religious histories.

To some, the Bible is on the same plane. Accepting it as a record of God's dealing with humanity as unfolded in historical narrative, they read it as one reads Emerson or Chaucer, taking from it moral ideas that serve as standards of human life and conduct. To them it is narrative. It is a textbook of life. It is not life itself, but a book about how to live life.

There are others who walk along the road of revelation to a deeper appreciation of the truth. To them the Bible lives. That is, they discover in the printed word an ever-unfolding understanding. They recognize that back of the printed page is a Spirit who can and does reveal the meaning of the Word. They read a chapter one day and rejoice in the revelation that it brings. A week later they discover a deeper truth hidden in the words they have read and the consciousness begins to dawn on them that the words they read a week ago are the media through which the Spirit of God approaches the heart and life. They discover there is a difference between the letters imprinted by the genius of the printer on a page of paper and the meaning of those letters unfolded and revealed by the Holy Spirit. For them, the Word begins to live.

Bible Revelations Never End

When we have mastered any other book in the world, we can lay it aside, for we have assimilated the knowledge that it reveals. When I went through my Euclid or Algebra in school days there was no need for me to go over and over them again to see if there was something I had missed. When I had mastered my Pons Assinoruin (the 5th problem of Euclid), it was conquered. I worked my problem. But not so with the Bible. We never exhaust its meaning. We never arrive at the finality of its riches. It is a living word in the sense that it means more than what it says on the page. One needs the Holy Spirit as a teacher to unfold its meaning and to impart the truth in power of which the words are only a representation.

In the third place, there are others who have been filled with the Spirit and who thereby have entered into the riches of a life that is hid with Christ in God. They have found the secret of the assimilation of the incarnate Word until it is translated into their own lives, and becomes strength and understanding and health of both body and soul. As the inspired Bible is the word of God on the printed page, it reveals the heart and mind and Word of the eternal.

Then came the day when that Word was made flesh. The purpose and mind and heart and plan of God were expressed in the miracle of the incarnation. Jesus Himself said, "He who has seen Me has seen the Father" (John 14:9). Not that Jesus was the Father. Rather He was the express image of the One who said, "You are My Son, Today I have begotten You" (Acts 13:33). So to know what God wants to do in the world, what He intends to do, what He will do through those who believe His Word, we have only to look at the life of Jesus and see what He did—and then read time and again His Words and believe them:

"Most assuredly, I say to you, he who believes in Me, the works that I do he will do also; and greater works than these he will do, because I go to My Father" (John 14:12).

Spiritual Power is Coming Again

Too often we look back to see what others have done and then let our heart and faith stay there. But we ought to go forward! The fullness of spiritual power is ahead. The completeness of the outpouring still awaits us. I believe that the richest and greatest experiences are just around the corner. The ark has not yet reached its destination. It is still coming our way.

In the economy of God, the plan of the divine works in cycles. The times of the Gentiles began with an image and it will close with an image. It began with a temple and it will close with one. This Church dispensation began with the upper room and it will finish with an upper room. It began with the presence of the power so poured out that sickness and suffering were swept away by the glory of the presence of the Lord. It will end the same way.

What happened then will happen again. The day is coming when the power of the Spirit will rest so mightily upon the hearts of Spirit-filled men and women that they will command blind eyes to open and they will obey instantly at the word. Power, God's power, Holy Spirit power, such as we have never known, will be poured out upon all consecrated flesh.

I believe Spirit-filled men and women will walk down hospital corridors, bringing relief to the sufferers and banishing disease in the name of the Lord. The day of revival is not over. Cities are yet to be shaken. The winds are to blow again in the tops of the mulberry trees. We have not yet received the fullness of the latter rain. We have not yet witnessed the full irresistible sweep of the power of the Holy Spirit and the majesty and victory of the indwelling Christ. But it is coming.

Obedience to the Word

The secret of power is obedience to the Word of God. For only as we obey can we be indwelt by His mighty presence. We must eat His flesh and drink His blood. We must be partakers of the divine nature. The words He spoke must be spirit and life to us. Then clothed with God and indwelt by His Spirit, Christians will march forward to glorious victory, radiant as an army with banners. The sick will be healed. Miracles of power and of glory that will bring heaven to earth will be done in the name of Jesus Christ.

Under the anointing of the Spirit the word of truth and power will be proclaimed. Under the urge of that indwelling life, every obstacle will give way and the world will see the greater things of which the Savior spoke. The prayer of intercession will be lost in the "hallelujah chorus" of praise. And Jesus, whom we preach and whom we receive, will be proclaimed Christ of all, the wisdom and the dynamite of God.

Greater Days Are Coming

The days of a carnal commandment are over. The days of allegiance to ceremonial laws have gone. This is the hour of the manifestation of the children of the Lord who have become partakers of the divine nature. This is the privilege of all who refuse to turn back, and who will know the glory and the blessing that comes from His indwelling—His presence will make your very blood throb with the power of an endless life. The multitude will follow Him for loaves and fishes. Others will follow after Him but afar off. But the little company of believers who are willing to pay the price and go with Him all the way will be the ones through whom the mighty power of the Spirit of God will manifest.

Be patient, be steadfast, greater days are ahead than we have ever seen.

FIVE

Be Patient and Steadfast

And He said to them, "Which of you shall have a friend, and go to him at midnight and say to him, 'Friend, lend me three loaves; 'for a friend of mine has come to me on his journey, and I have nothing to set before him;' and he will answer from within and say, 'Do not trouble me; the door is now shut, and my children are with me in bed; I cannot rise and give to you'? I say to you, though he will not rise and give to him because he is his friend, yet because of his persistence he will rise and give him as many as he needs" (Luke 11: 5-8).

Now He was telling them a parable to show that at all times they ought to pray and not to lose heart, ...
(Luke 18:1, NASB).

Be impatiently patient. Or as Smith Wigglesworth said, "Be satisfied with the satisfaction that is never satisfied." Never give up or be satisfied until you receive the answer promised you in the Word of God. The key word in prayer, in intercession, in ministering to others is "until." Pray, intercede, minister *until* you receive the answer you desire or the time for the answer has obviously passed—you're praying for a terminally ill person and the person dies. If this happens, don't be discouraged, don't be defeated, don't give up praying for the oppressed who need your help. Go on to the living and renew your efforts.

Many who pray often shut the door before the answer enters. They are like a marathon runner who quits and collapses exhausted by the wayside, not realizing that the finish line is just around the next bend — too taken up with the feelings within himself to even hear the cries of encouragement from those along the way who are urging him on — urging him to keep going, to keep trying, to finish the race.

God's Encouragers

For you, those encouragers "along the way" are God's angels sent to minister to you, just as to Jesus in the wilderness and in the Garden of Gethsemane.

> *And He was there in the wilderness forty days, tempted by Satan, and was with the wild beasts; and the angels ministered to Him* (Mark 1:13).

> *Then an angel appeared to Him from heaven, strengthening Him* (Luke 22:43).

> *Are they not all ministering spirits sent forth to minister for those who will inherit salvation?* (Hebrews 1:14)

You are never alone in the battle — the forces of God are on your side, coming to your aid. Be patient and hold fast. Increase your understanding and encourage yourself with the story of Daniel. He prayed and ate no food he enjoyed for three full weeks (Daniel 10:2-3), and then an angel appeared and among other things gave him, and us, insight into what sometimes happens in heavenly places when a righteous person prays.

Then he said to me, "Do not fear, Daniel, for from the first day that you set your heart to understand, and to humble yourself before your God, your words were heard; and I have come because of your words.

"But the prince of the kingdom of Persia withstood me twenty-one days; and behold, Michael, one of the chief princes, came to help me, ... " (Daniel 10:12-13).

Be like Daniel, patient and steadfast, until the answer comes. Don't be like Peter who gave up walking on the water when he was so close to Jesus that the Lord had only to stretch out His hand to catch him. That close! and Peter gave up. Be a Daniel, not a Peter.

Sometimes there are vast cosmic battles to be fought — the sending of angels to encourage, strengthen, and protect you (see **Lake's Protection from an Accident** and **A Story of Protection** at the end of this chapter). When you begin to seek power to destroy the enemy's works and set the oppressed free, you often stir up strong spiritual resistance. Sometimes you may feel like you're trying to fight an unbeatable foe, climb an unclimbable mountain, breathe air almost too thick to breathe.

When this happens, know that it is because the battle has been joined, that it is a sign that the enemy fears the power that you are seeking, and is determined to do all he can to discourage you from reaching your goal. I said, " ... discourage you," rather than " ... stop you" because stop you he cannot. He is already a defeated foe and can only put seemingly impossible obstacles in your path and try to bluff you into thinking that the battle will be too fierce, too long, and the obstacles too great for you to ever reach your goal of healing the oppressed and bringing glory to Jesus Christ.

But it is all smoke and shadows. He is a liar and the father of lies (John 8:44). The only real power he has is the power to deceive.

> *And war broke out in heaven: Michael and his angels fought with the dragon; and the dragon and his angels fought, but they did not prevail, nor was a place found for them in heaven any longer. So the great dragon was cast out, that serpent of old, called the Devil and Satan, who deceives the whole world; he was cast to the earth, and his angels were cast out with him* (Revelation 12:7-9).

So be patient and steadfast and stay the course until the Lord imparts to you the spiritual help you need. And impart it to you He will—for whenever you do not have enough of whatever you need to do whatever the Lord wants to do through you, He will always give you of what He has, if you will trust Him for it.

Smith Wigglesworth said, "Whenever I came to the end of my faith and it was not enough, I would storm heaven until I got hold of Him whose faith is always enough—and when I came back down I would have a faith that could not be denied."

Lake Receives Compassion from the Lord

Once in South Africa, we were praying for a sick lady, for a time without result. Then I said, "I will take my sister and go pray for her." We prayed again, and there was no victory.

A day or two afterwards my sister and I were in the city in one of the large department stores. As we stood

there the Spirit of the Lord said to me, "Go to her now."
I said to my sister, "As soon as you are through, we will
go over and pray for that sick lady."

We went, and I watched her writhe in pain and agony
until I put my arms about her and cuddled her head close
to my heart. Soon something broke loose in my soul,
and then in one moment (I hadn't even started to pray
yet) she was lifted out of her agony and suffering. A
divine flood moved her, and I knew she was healed. I
laid her down on the bed, took my sister's arm, and we
went away praising God.

I knew a man in South Africa who was an ardent
Methodist. He had ten sons, all Methodist preachers and
three beautiful daughters who were holy women. This
family was one of the most wonderful families I have
ever known. The old father had been stricken with
disease, and the agony of his suffering was so great that
the only way to relieve him was to drug him into
insensibility. As the years passed, he became a morphine
addict. He told me that he smoked 24 cigars, drank two
quarts of whiskey, and used a tremendous quantity of
morphine every day. The old man, 73 years old, was
drugged into senselessness most of the time.

I prayed with him unceasingly for sixteen hours
without result. William Duggin, one of my ministers,
hearing of the situation, came to my assistance. He stood
over the old gentleman and prayed for him in the power
of God, but somehow there was no answer. I watched
that man in convulsions until his daughters begged me
to let them give him a little morphine and die senseless,
rather than to let him suffer longer. I said, "No. I have
had your pledge and his, too, that life or death, we are
going to fight this battle through."

Presently as I stood there watching the awful
convulsions, the Scripture came to my mind, "Himself

took our infirmities" (Matthew 8:17). I reached out and got hold of him and held him as in a grip of iron. A compassion that is too deep for any form of expression we know broke forth in my soul; and in a single moment I saw him lie still, healed by God's power.

Many a day after that I have walked with him over his three vast estates, on which there were 50,000 orange trees and 50,000 lemon trees. As we walked the old man told me of his love for God and of the richness of His presence, and I have my reward.

If the church ever succeeds in doing that which God purposes we should do, it can only be when we enter into that divine compassion of the Son of God.

The Enemy's Weapons

Deception, doubt, discouragement, fears—these are the enemy's most effective weapons, but the Word of God is a sharp, two-edged, sword that will cut through them all. Armed with the breastplate of righteousness, the shield of faith, and the sword of the Word you will win every battle, even though you may get a bit bloodied now and then.

Blumhardt's Battle

Bishop Johann Christopher Blumhardt was a pastor in Möttlingen, a small village in Württemberg, Germany, who in the 19th century developed almost as much spiritual power as John G. Lake did in the 20th century. He fought a two-year battle over the mind and body of a young woman, Gottliebin Dittus, who suffered from a range of strange illnesses and problems. As Blumhardt ministered to her, she manifested signs of possession. Why she was tormented in this way is uncertain, but she had been involved in magical practices that were common with villagers at that time, and that may have been the doorway for the possessing spirits—thousands of them apparently.

Many prominent officials in the village and in Blumhardt's denomination counseled him to stay away from such things and leave Gottliebin to God - the local doctor had given up on her - but Blumhardt refused to do so. Thus began an intensive two-year spiritual battle, one in which Blumhardt sometimes was the only one who believed the Lord could win. Often he was called out at night to witness the most horrifying symptoms - and always he stayed and prayed until Gottliebin was relieved.

Blumhardt refused all superstitious healing techniques and methods and relied solely upon Jesus' victory on the Cross and the Word of God. Once he was told through Gottliebin that the spirits often wanted to attack him, and if he had turned once from the Word of God to man's ways, they would have been able to.

Spirit after spirit left Gottliebin over the two-year's of the battle until the weakened final spirit within Gottliebin screamed in a voice heard several houses away, "Jesus is Victor," and departed. Almost immediately, revival broke out in the village and hundreds were converted to Jesus Christ. Gottliebin recovered completely, and for the rest of her life was devoted to Bishop Blumhardt and his wife and took care of their house and children.

This two-year battle launched Blumhardt into a healing ministry that was so effective he established a healing home at a spa called Bad Boll, about a 20-minute walk from a village of the same name. There he ministered to thousands who came from all over the world. Blumhardt often said, "Healing is nothing more than the very real presence of Jesus Christ." Throughout the years of his healing ministry, Blumhardt relied solely upon Jesus' victory on the Cross and the Word of God.

Many Who Minister Today

Many who minister to the sick and oppressed today are neither patient nor steadfast, and are prideful in their belief in the amount of spiritual power they have. They pray once and send the sick away to struggle on their own to have and maintain the faith needed to overcome their sickness. But if God does not impart faith, it is virtually impossible for a sick person to do that, as anyone who has had a serious physical, mental, or emotional problem will testify. The responsibility for steadfastness, patience, and continued ministry belongs to those who minister to the sick.

A minister to whom this was once said, responded, "I'm not going to take the responsibility for healing someone. That's too much of a burden and I'm not going to carry it. I pray once for them and then it's up to them and God. It's no longer my responsibility."

But what kind of a doctor would it be who sent you away with a prescription for one dose of medicine and told you not to come back again, that he had done his part and now your healing was up to you? He would be considered the worst kind of doctor and really not a doctor at all. Yet, that is what many do who claim to have the faith and power—or anointing as so many call it—to heal others. They pray once with their great faith and when nothing happens send the sick on their way with the admonition to "Just believe"—but don't come again for prayer because they have "prayed the prayer of faith" over you.

Not so with John G. Lake. At his healing home in Spokane, Washington, he insisted that the sick person be prayed for as many times as necessary until their healing manifested, even if it took hours or days or weeks of prayer and laying on of hands.

Ministered to Thirty Times

Mr. W. A. Fay suffered from cancer of the stomach. He has been ministered to perhaps thirty times.

For the first ten days, there was no evidence of healing whatever or a subsiding of his suffering. After that, there was a gradual subsiding; then color began to return to his face, and he began to put on flesh.

Now he can eat anything and everything, and as much of it as he can get! And that is not all, beloved. He found the Lord and Savior Jesus Christ while the process was going on, and he says that is the big part of it.

I guess the Lord knows how to open doors in people's hearts. A good many Christians overlook the fact that Jesus Christ made the ministry of healing just as broad as He could make it.

To the Seventy (Luke 10:8-9), He said, " … *into whatsoever city ye enter, and they receive you … heal the sick that are therein.*" And then what did He tell them to do? "… *Say unto them, The kingdom of God is come nigh unto you.*"

Battled Cancer for Months

Last evening in the healing rooms, just at six o'clock, I was visited by a woman who I met four or five months ago in the Deaconess Hospital. The dear lady had been given up to die. She had been examined by x-ray, and a large cancer in her stomach was discovered. They told her there was nothing to be done for her. So the dear husband sent for me to speak a kindly word to his supposedly dying wife. I did not understand what I had been sent for and when I got to the dear soul, I supposed I had been called to pray the prayer of faith for healing.

I said, "Dear Mother, you do not have to die."

"But," she said, "the doctor says so. The X-ray shows such a sized cancer. I guess, brother, I will have to die."

And I said, "It is a lie. You do not have to die."

For two or three months, we battled against that condition in the woman's soul. The Spirit of God would come upon her every time we prayed. Her pains would disappear, she would go to sleep, etc., but she was not really healed. *That went on week after week and month after month until I was almost worn out before her soul raised to take victory.*

But last night she *walked* into the healing rooms. She told me that she weighed only seventy-five pounds when I met her and that now she weighs one hundred twenty pounds. She went to the hospital this week and had the same physician x-ray her. When they saw the picture, they said, "There must be some mistake." And they got the original and examined it. They could not understand it.

She said, "Doctor, I found a new Physician, the Great Physician, the Christ of God, and I do not care about your [x-ray] plates. I know the cancer is gone."

But the [x-ray] plates showed it was gone. The woman has gone back home a happy woman. But, beloved, the victory only came when the consciousness of the power of the living Christ took possession of that woman's heart. Blessed be God.

Not a dead Jesus, but a living Christ! Not a sepulcher with a dead man in it, but the glorious, risen, present Christ in your heart and mine. The Christ lives, bless God, at not only the right hand of God, but the Christ lives in your soul and mine. The victory that He attained is evidenced not alone by the declaration: *"I am he that liveth, and was dead; and, behold, I am alive for evermore,"* but the victory He attains through you and me now.

That was His peculiar victory, but the victory of the Christ that gives the [children] of God [their] gladness now is the consciousness that the Christ lives and the Christ reigns and that by the power of God, sin, darkness, death, and hell become obedient to the Christians through the Christ that is in [them].

Ministered to Four Times

Mrs. Carter is one of my neighbors. She lives at 714 South Sherman, [Spokane, Washington]. Mrs. Carter had a tumor. For nine months, her physicians believed that the woman was pregnant, until after nature's time had passed.

She continued to grow larger and larger for thirteen months from the beginning, until it was estimated that the tumor would weigh fifteen pounds. She came to the healing rooms and I ministered to her on three occasions, when there seemed to be no special evidence of healing beyond that her body relaxed and became comfortable.

But the fourth time she was ministered to, the Spirit of the Lord came upon her so powerfully that the next morning she returned at eleven o'clock perfectly normal in size. The tumor had disappeared—not as tumors usually do, in liquid form, or giving any sign of substance whatever. It simply dematerialized and disappeared and was gone. God Almighty did it, bless His name!

When I stand in the presence of people like Mrs. Carter and realize what God has done in them, it seems to me that if I had been suddenly brought face-to-face with such things [for] the first time, an awe of God would get hold of my soul as it did twenty-five years ago when for the first time I saw God heal people.

Lake's Brother Healed at Alexander Dowie's Meeting

Twenty-five years ago, this ministry was as new to me as it is to you. I went into one of John Alexander Dowie's great meetings in Chicago where a portion of the room was filled with cots on which dying folks lay. My brother, a man who had been an invalid for twenty-two years and the most terrible sufferer I have ever seen, was healed in that room.

Dowie came in and sat down to teach for a little while, and as he looked down and saw the intense suffering of my brother, he dropped his Bible and came down to him and said, "Young fellow, I see you are suffering," and he prayed for him. Instantly the power of God flashed through him. He arose and walked out of the place in his nightgown.

Three others, a great deal like him, were on cots. Dowie prayed for each one, and one after another received the healing touch and arose from their cots. When I saw [my brother] well, I walked on my tiptoes for about three weeks. The wonder of God's power had been revealed to my Methodist soul.

Any Church Can Have Healing Power

In a church where there is a steadfast emphasis on the need to be born again by the Spirit of God, there will be true salvations.

In a church where there is a steadfast emphasis on sanctification—separation from the world unto God—and holiness, there will be separation and holiness.

In a church where there is a steadfast emphasis on the authority of Jesus' name and the power of the Holy Spirit to heal, there will be healings. All that is needed is for the leaders of the church to develop an atmosphere of faith throughout the congregation. It is the atmosphere of faith that results in healings like those in the miracle meetings of Kathryn Kuhlman, John G. Lake, Charles Price, and others—not some special anointing on the person on the platform. "Where two or three are gathered together [in faith in My name], I am there in the midst of them [to do signs and wonders]" (Matthew 18:20).

The relationship between what is patiently and steadfastly taught in a church and what is manifested is that direct and that simple. It is the same in the life of an individual. So be patient and steadfast and continually move toward your goal of obtaining the spiritual power you need to heal the sick and free the oppressed.

Lake's Protection from an Accident

What about accidents? Does the Holy Spirit, in His leading and guiding you, lead you into an accident that would tear up and break up the temple in which He dwells'? Your body is the temple of the Holy Spirit. Your body was bought by God and belongs to Him (1 Corinthians 6:19-20). Psalm 91 gives promise of protection from the plague and pestilence. It also shows we need not fear the arrow that flies by day. This is the hunter's promise of protection. This Psalm also states that we should not be afraid of the destruction that lays waste at noonday. "For He shall give His angels charge over you, To keep you in all your ways. In their hands they shall bear you up, Lest you dash your foot against a stone" (Psalm 91:11-12).

Angels are "ministering spirits sent forth to minister for those who will inherit salvation" (Hebrews 1:14). Angels are involved in a ministry of protection. So it is obvious that God wants to and will protect your body from accidents. The Holy Spirit will not lead you into an accident, but will prevent it if you are sensitive to His voice.

As I was coming up one of the mountain highways that we have here, a voice said to me, "Pull on to the left of the road and stop."

Do you know that voice, Christian heart? That voice is so common that I never even spoke of it to my wife and haven't spoken to her about it yet. I have listened to that voice so long and for so many years that I have learned to obey the voice of the Lord. "My sheep hear My voice" (John 10:27).

The thought I am trying to bring to you, dear friends, is the value of knowing the Lord, what communion with God means. Salvation is not just something that God gives that is going to bless you after you die—it is having the presence of the Lord now. And, dear friends, God has promised to the Christian the guidance and direction of the Holy Spirit.

Very well, I pulled onto the left-hand side of the road and ran my wheels close to the ditch and stopped. Presently I heard the grinding of a great truck coming down around the curve, that I had not seen before. Instead of coming normally, it was coming down the left-hand side of the road at an angle of forty-five degrees. The thing had gotten out of control on the steep hill, and was covering the whole road.

If I had been on my own side of the road, it would have sideswiped me and pushed me over the bank a hundred feet or more down. It was on the other side of the road and the great thing just went past me, went down a little ways, fifty or one hundred feet past me, struck a rough spot in the road, and righted itself. The driver then got the truck under control and went on.

Listen, dear friends, men and women in this Word of God were guided by the voice of God. God talked to them. That is the inner thing of real Christian experience. That is the reason real Christians seek by the grace of God to enter into the real heart of God, into the real soul of Jesus Christ, into the place where He lives within you, where His voice speaks in your heart.

A Story of Protection

A woman brought her brother, Carl, to her pastorwhom we'll call Steve. Carl was under court order to either get counseling for alcoholism or serve a jail sentence.

The jail sentence was imposed because when Carl drank he frequently became violent. Often he would wake up in the morning with his knuckles or face or both bruised and bloody but with no idea of what had happened to him until others told him. Several times, he woke up in jail, and in his last violent episode, it had taken six police officers to subdue him.

Although Steve did not counsel alcoholics, he had been ministering to the sick and oppressed for some time and had developed a fair amount of power in certain areas. The woman believed her brother's problem was in one of those areas.

The ministering took place in the upper room of an old building where the church met. After introducing her brother, Carl, to Steve, the woman went downstairs to pray, leaving her brother and pastor alone.

During their initial conversation, it was obvious to Steve that Carl had been drinking, and Carl admitted having "a couple of beers" to fortify himself. He was a personable young man, about 35, medium height, stocky, with long black hair and a black beard—and visibly nervous. It was also obvious that Carl was not a Christian, although he thought he "might be one."

After talking to Carl for a while about his need for Jesus Christ and that only Jesus could set him free from the bondage of alcoholism, Steve asked him, "Do you want to receive Jesus Christ as your Lord and Savior?"

Carl said, "Yes."

They had been sitting in the congregation area, and for a reason that Steve cannot now explain he took Carl up onto a low platform where the speaker stand was, turned two metal chairs around in front of a window overlooking a street, and had Carl kneel at one of them while he knelt at the other one next to him. Then he said, "Carl, just talk to Jesus. Tell him you're sorry for your sins, that you need His help, and ask Him to be your Lord and Savior." He then started praying silently for Carl.

Carl leaned on the chair with his forearms crossed over the seat—his head was bent forward, and his hair hung down over the sides of his face. He was silent for a minute or two, then began to moan, softly at first and then louder and louder. This went on for about another minute or so and then the moans turned into a sharp, guttural, sound and he began to slam his right forearm down on the chair seat.

Not yet aware of the unexpected thing that had happened, and thinking Carl was having a struggle in his salvation prayer, Steve moved closer to him and put his left hand on Carl's shoulder to encourage him. When he did, Carl's head came up and he twisted on his knees to face Steve. His hair hung down over his face, now about twenty-four inches from Steve's face, and what glared out of Carl's eyes was not Carl. It was a complete Jekyll and Hyde transformation.

"At that instant," Steve relates, "God poured grace upon me and filled me with His Holy Spirit and faith. So much so, that I was amazed when the first words out of my mouth were, 'Well, where did you come from?' I felt absolutely no concern or fear—and was as peaceful inside as any human being can be."

Carl, however, or what was now possessing Carl, was not at peace. Pure hate and evil glared out through Carl's eyes, and he hunched forward toward Steve, growling and snarling like a wild animal about to attack.

Steve said he then heard himself say, "You don't frighten me—your kind couldn't touch Jesus and you can't touch me because Christ lives in me. And wherever you came from, you can't remain in Carl, so come out of him in the name of Jesus Christ!"

For a moment a look of uncertainty flashed in Carl's eyes, and then he raised his arms, hands extended like hooks, and reached forward for Steve's throat. Steve logically should have backed away from him or tried to grab his arms, but instead he heard himself say, "What do you think you're going to do? I told you, you can't touch me anymore than you could touch Jesus Christ!"

Carl's hands moved to about six inches from Steve's throat and stopped. The cords in his neck stood out and his hands began to shake violently as the spirit in him strained against some invisible barrier to reach Steve.

"You can't touch me," Steve said again. "Jesus Christ is My Lord and He defeated your master two-thousand years ago. Now come out of Carl in the name of Jesus Christ!"

Although still straining to reach Steve's throat, uncertainty flooded Carl's eyes and he turned his head to one side, away from looking at Steve.

Still astonished at his total lack of fear and absolute certain of his power over the spirit in Carl, Steve reached up with his right hand through Carl's still extended arms and grabbed his chin and forced his head back toward him.

"Don't turn your head away from me," he said. "Look into my eyes and see Jesus Christ in me and come out of Carl!"

When they were fully face-to-face again, Steve said that the look in Carl's eyes had turned to total fear. Then in what seemed to be a desperate effort, Carl lunged forward until the tips of his fingers touched Steve's throat.

"Amazingly," Steve said, "I still felt no fear. And then this look of utter bewilderment came over Carl's face, and his arms, still fully extended, began to move downward—slowly, smoothly, like fluid, even though he was straining to keep them up.

"The spirit was using every muscle in Carl's body to try to hold his arms up, but they kept moving down, away from me. I was as bewildered by it all as he looked, but also totally fascinated as I watched it. And what happened next blew me away!

"Carl's arms were still fully extended, and when they reached his sides they kept right on going behind him, like they were being pulled backwards. At that moment, though it may have just been my imagination, I had the distinct impression that this very large angel had taken hold of Carl's arms when his fingers touched my throat and pulled them down and away from me.

"Whether that was true or not, I don't know, but Carl's arms continued to be pulled backwards until his body was also pulled back and he fell to the floor. All this time, the look in his eyes was a combination of pure fear and desperation."

When Carl fell to the floor, the spirit temporarily released him and Carl reappeared. Finding himself on the floor and away from the chair where he had been kneeling, Carl's first words to Steve were, "What did you do to me?"

Steve told him what had happened, and explained to him the connection between the demon in him and his alcoholism. A few minutes later the spirit repossessed Carl in a last ditch effort to remain in him but it was all bluff and bluster and it soon came out permanently in the name of Jesus Christ. When it did, Carl was free and instantly healed of his alcoholism.

SIX

Be Full of Faith, the Holy Spirit, and Power

Immediately the fountain of her blood was dried up, and she felt in her body that she was healed of the affliction. And Jesus, immediately knowing in Himself that power had gone out of Him, turned around in the crowd and said, "Who touched My clothes?" (Mark 5:29-30)

"Therefore, brethren, seek out from among you seven men of good reputation, full of the Holy Spirit and wisdom," ... they chose Stephen, a man full of faith and the Holy Spirit, ... And Stephen, full of faith and power, did great wonders and signs among the people (Acts 6:3, 5, 8).

Sometimes it is not a whole Bible verse that inspires and encourages you, but part of one. About thirty years ago when I was constantly reading in the Bible and in every book I could find about all the possibilities of faith, I was more discouraged than helped because of the weakness of my faith at that time. Then I read the beginning of Romans 10:17, "So then faith comes ..." Ah, I thought, no matter how weak my faith is now, no matter how ineffective it is, it will become stronger and more effective as I study and meditate on the Word of God—because "faith comes."

Faith, the Holy Spirit, and power are three essentials for healing the oppressed. Peter said to Cornelius the Centurion, " ... *God anointed Jesus of Nazareth with the Holy Spirit and with power, [and He] went about doing good and healing all who were oppressed by the devil, for God was with Him."* Now if Jesus needed the Holy Spirit and power to heal the sick and free the oppressed, then we certainly do also.

Jesus' faith in God—and faith is always in someone or something—is never mentioned in the Scriptures, but in Luke 4:1 it says of Him, "Then Jesus, being filled with the Holy Spirit, ... was led by the Spirit into the wilderness." And Luke 4:14 says, "Then Jesus returned in the power of the Spirit to Galilee, and news of Him went out through all the surrounding region." He went into the wilderness "filled with the Holy Spirit" and came out of it forty days later in the "power of the Spirit."

Mark's version of the Luke 4:1 incident puts it more directly, and by so doing gives us added insight into how the Holy Spirit works with us at times: "Immediately the Spirit drove Him into the wilderness" (Mark 1:12). The Amplified Bible (AMP) helps us to further understand by putting it this way: "Immediately the [Holy] Spirit [from within] drove Him into the wilderness." So as you progress in your quest for spiritual power, you can expect at times an inward driving of the Holy Spirit to accomplish a task that God wants to do through you.

In Mark 11:23 Jesus speaks of what we might call mountain-moving faith and what it can do. Some insist that a person can acquire such faith. But with a bit of spiritual logic we can easily understand why God would not allow a person to have such faith, and why He would not impart mountain-moving faith without a filling of the Holy Spirit—thereby keeping the faith under the control of the Holy Spirit.

If you had mountain-moving faith, and I had mountain-moving faith, and Joe and Jane Christian each had it, you would move the mountain to one place, I would move it to another, and Joe and Jane would each move it to another place. We would create complete spiritual chaos. And if we were given such faith without also being filled with the Holy Spirit, few of us would move the mountain to where God wanted it moved, and so God's work and the kingdom of His beloved Son would not be advanced.

Without getting into theological or doctrinal controversies about physical manifestations or spiritual gifts, the essential meaning of being filled with, or the state of being full of, the Holy Spirit is to be *controlled by the Holy Spirit.*

So to seek out someone who is "full of the Holy Spirit" as they did with Stephen is to seek out someone whose words and actions demonstrate he is constantly controlled and motivated by the Holy Spirit. That's the meaning of the verse in Mark 1:12, especially as given in the Amplified Bible. The Holy Spirit drove Jesus from within into the wilderness. In other words, Jesus being full of, or filled with, the Holy Spirit (Luke 4:1) was controlled by the Holy Spirit.

Some have referred to this as "the Spirit of God falling upon them," or "being moved upon by the Holy Spirit," or the "Holy Spirit coming upon them." It is all the same thing.

We will look at some instances of this in Dr. Lake's life in just a moment. But first, what will be the effects of this upon you when God wants you to do something that He wants done? Some of the effects are that you will sometimes find yourself doing something without knowing why you are doing it, knowing things that you had no way of knowing, saying things that you had not thought of saying, or having a faith that has absolutely no unbelief in it—or a combination of all of them.

Previously BrokenArm Lengthens Four Inches

The Sunday night meetings of the pastor whom we're calling Steve had developed a fair amount of power. They were held in the upper room of an old building where the church met. Only about 25 people attended the morning service, but about 100 crowded into the upper room in the evening meeting, which ran from seven until sometimes after midnight.

After one of the morning services, a member of his congregation, Alice, asked him to pray for her left arm during the evening meeting.

"What's wrong with it?" Steve asked.

"I fell and broke my elbow about fifteen years ago, and it was several days before I could get to a doctor. By then the broken bones had begun to set themselves, and he said the only way he could fix my arm was to re-break the elbow bones, which he advised against. So ever since then my left arm has been four inches shorter than my right arm."

With that, Alice held her arms straight out in front of her with the palms of her hands together. The finger tips on her left hand came to just inside the base of the thumb on her right hand.

Steve looked at the difference in the length of her arms, thought of how long they had been that way, then looked inside himself and said, "I'm sorry, Alice, but I just don't have the faith to pray for an arm that much shorter than the other, especially since it would mean that either your elbow would have to be healed or the arm itself would have to be lengthened. Sorry."

Alice dropped her arms, said, "That's okay," and walked away.

Steve could feel her disappointment, but he still knew he did not have the faith to pray for an arm like that.

That evening the power in the upper room was so strong it seemed to thicken the air. Like on all Sunday evenings the meeting started with everyone sitting in a large circle three rows deep and singing songs of praise and worship. And like on so many of those evenings, something in the air suddenly changed, like there was someone there who had not been there before. Steve could always feel it when it happened, and usually there would be sudden manifestations of power around the room. Steve and his wife and a few selected others would then begin to minister to the sick and oppressed.

After about thirty minutes of ministering on this particular evening, Steve saw Alice and her husband, Ken, sitting in the front row on the left side of the room. He went over to them and said to Alice, "Alice, stand up, Jesus is going to heal your arm."

He had her stretch her arms out as she had that morning and held his left arm our straight in front of her and had her rest her forearms on his left forearm. Then he turned her at a slight angle to the room and called out, "Everybody, stop what you're doing and look at this. All you young people look at this! I want everyone to see this. Alice's left arm is almost four inches short, she broke her elbow fifteen years ago, and Jesus is going to lengthen her arm right now. Everybody watch this!"

Then he prayed, "Lord Jesus, give yourself honor and glory—lengthen this arm. In the name of Jesus Christ of

Nazareth I command this left arm to be healed and be the same length as the right arm." The left hand instantly started moving forward. There were gasps and shouts of praise all over the room.

In not more than a minute the left arm moved slowly and smoothly outward until it was the same length as the right arm. During the entire process Steve had total faith that the arm was going to be healed – there was not a speck of doubt anywhere in him. Yet, that morning he was all doubt without a speck of faith.

Lake Controlled and Led by the Holy Spirit

You can see this type of Holy Spirit control and guidance in several instances in John G. Lake's ministry.

While still in Indianapolis, Indiana, before going to South Africa, Lake had been praying about a specific kind of spiritual power for some months. As you read how he received it, note the controlling or driving force within him.

Fasting and Prayer Imposed by the Holy Spirit

One morning when I came down to breakfast I found my appetite had disappeared. I could not eat. I went about my work as usual. At dinner, I had no desire to eat, and no more in the evening. This went on till the third day. But toward the evening of the third day, an overwhelming desire to pray took possession of me. I wanted only to be alone to pray.

Prayer flowed from my soul like a stream. I could not cease praying. As soon as it was possible to get to a place of seclusion, I would kneel to pour out my heart to God for hours. Whatever I was doing, that stream of prayer continued flowing from my soul.

On the night of the sixth day of this fast that the Lord had laid on me, while in the act of washing my hands, the Spirit said to me once again, "Go and pray." I turned around and knelt by my bedside.

As I knelt praying, the Spirit said, "How long have you been praying to cast out demons?" and I replied, "Lord, a long time." And the Spirit said, "From henceforth you shall cast out demons." I arose and praised God.

The Flame of God

After returning from Africa some years ago, I spent some time visiting my brother and my sister. As we sat together one day, my sister said, John, I have some neighbors here who are elderly German people and they are having a very hard time.

"First, the old man died; then one of the sisters died. This thing happened and that thing happened. Finally, the son, who is a shipbuilder, fell and was carried to the hospital. Now gangrene has set in; they say his leg has to be amputated.

"The old mother, a rheumatic cripple, has been sitting in a wheelchair for two and a half years and cannot move."

My brother and I had been having a discussion over this very thing. Jim, a splendid fellow and a professor and well-educated, said, "John, don't you think these things are all psychological?'

"Not much," I said.

He said. "I think it is. Don't you think healing is a demonstration of the power of mind over matter?"

I said, "No. If that were all it is, you could give just as good a demonstration as I could."

After awhile, our sister said, "I have been across the street and have made arrangements for you to go and pray for these people."

I said, "All right. Jim, come along."

When we arrived, I asked the old lady, "Mother, how long have you been in this wheelchair?"

She replied. "Two and a half years. It is awful hard. Not just hard sitting here all the time, but I suffer night and day, with no moment of relaxation from my acute suffering for all this time."

As I listened to her, the flame of God came into my soul. I said, "You rheumatic devil, in the name of Jesus Christ, I will blot you out, if it is the last thing I ever do in the world!" Laying hands on her, I looked to Heaven and called on God to cast that devil out and set her free.

Then I said to her, "Mother, in the name of Jesus Christ, get out of your chair and walk!"

And she arose and walked!

My brother said, "My, it beats the devil."

I replied, "That's the intention!"

Holy Spirit Uses a Six-Year-Old Child

In the Word of God, men and women were guided by the Voice of God. God talked to them. This is the inner thing of real Christian experience, the reason to seek by the grace of God to enter into the real heart of God—into the real soul of Jesus Christ—into the place where He lives within you—where His Voice speaks in your heart.

I was sitting one day in the home of the DeValeras in Krugersdorp, South Africa, when a man arrived who had traveled all over the country. He had been following me from place to place, trying to catch up with me. He suffered a sunstroke that had affected his mind and he also developed a large cancer. He was a friend of the family and came into the house and told me his story.

After awhile, a six-year-old child who had been sitting near me went across the room, climbed on the man's knees, put her hands on the cancer on his face, and prayed.

Beloved, I saw the cancer wither. In half an hour, the thing had disappeared. The wound was still there, but in a few days, it was healed.

After the child had laid her hands on top of his head, he arose, saying, "Oh! The fire that has been in my brain has gone out," and his mind was normal.

"Power belongs to God" (Psalm 62:11). The simplest soul can touch God and live in the very presence of God and in His power.

It is almost a sadness to my soul that so many Christians should be astonished and surprised at an ordinary, tangible, evidence of the power of God.

We have not yet learned to keep in living touch with the powers of God. Once in awhile our souls rise, and we see the flame of God accomplish this wonder and that. But, beloved, Jesus Christ lived in the presence of God every hour of the day and night. Never a word proceeded from the mouth of Jesus Christ, but that which was God's Word. He said, "The words that I speak to you are spirit, and they are life." (John 6:63).

When you and I are lost in the Son of God and the fires of Jesus burn in our hearts, as they did in His, our words will be the words of Spirit and of life. There will be no death in them. Beloved, we are on the way.

Is this filling and control of the Holy Spirit essential for every healing? No, many healings can be accomplished without it as your faith in the name of Jesus Christ increases.

But it *is* essential for those special things that God wants to do through you, and those times when you absolutely need the Holy Spirit to come upon you for a healing that would not take place without it.

Groin Pain Healed Before Surgery

The same pastor, Steve, and his wife were invited by an evangelist friend to attend three days of evangelistic meetings at a church in Kentucky. The evangelist, who was also a musician, traveled with his wife, sister, and brother-in-law. All except the brother-in-law were musicians and gospel singers—he handled their sound system.

On the second afternoon of the meetings, they were all relaxing near the motel's swimming pool. There was a tennis court, and the brother-in-law, whom we'll call Ralph, and his wife were playing tennis. Suddenly Ralph doubled over in apparent pain. Everyone went to him and after a few minutes his pain lessened and his wife and the evangelist helped him back into his motel room.

Steve asked the evangelist's wife what was wrong with Ralph. "He gets sudden, excruciating, pains in his groin," she said. "He's been examined by several doctors and x-rayed but they can't find anything wrong with him. It's getting worse, so next week he's going into the hospital for an exploratory operation to see if they can find what's causing the pain."

That evening, just before the start of the meeting, Steve and his wife were sitting in the front row. The evangelist came out from a room behind the platform and motioned to them. They went over to him and he said, "Ralph is having terrible pains and we're going to pray for him and want you two to join us."

In the backroom, the pastor of the church told everyone to gather around Ralph and lay hands on him. They did, except for Steve, and the pastor began to pray for Jesus to relieve Ralph's pain. Steve always felt awkward about joining with several others to lay hands on someone, and so he stayed a few feet behind the pastor and prayer silently.

Then, as Steve tells it, the strangest thing happened. He went up behind the pastor, put his hand on his shoulder, pushed him gently to one side—interrupting his prayer—and said, "Let me pray for him."

"I faintly remember seeing shocked looks on everyone's face," Steve says in recalling the incident, "especially the pastor's. I'm not certain but what I felt almost as shocked as he looked because this was something I had never done before, or would have ever thought of doing. Yet at the same time it seemed to be the most natural thing to do."

Then, somehow knowing within himself everything that was going to happen, Steve said to Ralph, "I'm going to lay my hands on each side of your groin and command a constricting spirit to come out. When I do, the pain is going to get worse, but just hang on because that thing is going to come out."

Ralph looked as puzzled as everyone else, but grabbed Steve's arms and nodded his head, his face already twisting in pain.

Steve positioned his hands on Ralph and said, "All right, you foul constricting spirit, you have no right to torment a child of God, so come out of him in the name of Jesus Christ." At that, Ralph gasped and moaned in pain and bent forward until his head rested on Steve's chest.

As the pain in Ralph increased, Steve said he had a mental image, though he admits it may have just been his imagination, of tentacles tightening and squeezing Ralph in the area of pain—trying to hang on. He commanded again, "Loose those tentacles and release this child of God and come out of him in the name of Jesus Christ!"

Through all of this, Steve said, he never had a moment's doubt that the spirit was going to come out. He was, in Steve's words, "All faith and certainty."

The battle continued for about another minute with Ralph moaning louder and louder. Then when another command was given for the constricting spirit to come out, he suddenly stopped moaning, was silent for a moment, and then said, "Praise the Lord! Thank You, Jesus!" and straightened up, free of pain.

When he and his wife returned home, he cancelled the exploratory operation. The pain never returned. *

In Mark 16:17-18, it's recorded that Jesus said, " ... these signs will follow those who believe: In My name they will cast out demons; ... they will lay hands on the sick, and they will recover."

In this I have long agreed with Smith Wigglesworth who re-punctuated verse 17 so that the two verses read, " ... these signs will follow those who believe in My name: they will cast out demons; ... they will lay hands on the sick, and they will recover."

Signs do not follow Christians who simply believe in Him, they follow Christians who believe in His name, in the authority and power of His name. This is so obvious in practice that it cannot be disputed.

This agrees with what Peter said after he and John had healed the man at the Gate Beautiful and everybody wanted

---

* Dr. Charles S. Price, a Methodist minister whom God used in a mighty healing ministry for thirty years, wrote a marvelous book about imparted faith: *The Real Faith for Healing*. It's published by Bridge-Logos Publishers. Every Christian interested in healing others or needing healing should study it.

to give them the credit. What he said speaks not only of what faith in the name of Jesus Christ will accomplish, but also of faith in Jesus' name being imparted.

> *... why look so intently at us, as though by our own power or godliness we had made this man walk? The God of Abraham, Isaac, and Jacob, the God of our fathers, glorified His Servant Jesus, ... And His name, through faith in His name, has made this man strong, whom you see and know. Yes, the faith which comes through Him has given him this perfect soundness in the presence of you all* (Acts 3:12, 13, 16).

He also emphasized this authority and power in the name of Jesus Christ to the rulers who questioned them about how they had healed the lame man.

> *If we this day are judged for a good deed done to a helpless man, by what means he has been made well, let it be known to you all, and to all the people of Israel, that by the name of Jesus Christ of Nazareth, whom you crucified, whom God raised from the dead, by Him this man stands here before you whole"* (Acts 4:9-10).

Faith to heal is not faith in healing itself—many believe strongly in divine healing and get no one healed. It is faith in the authority and healing power of the name of Jesus Christ.

> *All authority has been given to Me in heaven and on earth. Go therefore ...* (Matthew 28:18)

> *Then the seventy returned with joy, saying, "Lord, even the demons are subject to us in Your name"* (Luke 10:17).

The name of Jesus Christ is so powerful that someone who wasn't even a disciple of Jesus used it to cast out demons, thereby upsetting the Lord's chosen twelve. Notice also what the Lord called the casting out of demons—it's the only thing He ever identified as being a miracle.

> *Now John answered Him, saying, "Teacher, we saw someone who does not follow us casting out demons in Your name, and we forbade him because he does not follow us."*
>
> *But Jesus said, "Do not forbid him, for no one who works a miracle in My name can soon afterward speak evil of Me"* (Mark 9:38-39).

Since we know that the Word of God cannot be wrong, we know that faith in the Lord's name can be increased by meditating on the Word of God, *"Faith comes by hearing, and hearing by the Word of God,"* and by increasing experiences of the absolute authority of His name in the spiritual realm. As your faith in the authority of His name increases, you will find more and deeper healings taking place, and will experience more instances of the filling of the Holy Spirit and imparted faith for those particular things that God wants to do through you.

Praying in the Name of Jesus

Jesus called His twelve disciples and commanded upon them power and authority to cast out devils and heal disease (Luke 9:1). He superseded this later by declaring: "If you ask anything in My name, I will do it" (John 14:14).

The first was a limited power of attorney. The second, unlimited. This unlimited power of attorney was authorized before His crucifixion. It was to become effective when the Holy Spirit came.

On the Day of Pentecost, this power of attorney was made fully operative. The Spirit came. First, legally, they had His Word. Then, vitally, He sent His Spirit.

At the Gate Beautiful, Peter and John exercised the authority in Jesus' name. Passing into the temple, they met a beggar. He was forty years old and had been lame from his mother's womb. Peter commanded: "In the name of Jesus Christ of Nazareth, rise up and walk" (Acts 3:6). Heaven's lightning struck the man. He leaped to his feet, instantly healed.

A multitude rushed up. They demanded: "In what name, by what power, have you done this?" Then the religious took hold of them and demanded to know also.

Peter and John replied: "By the name of Jesus Christ of Nazareth, whom you crucified, whom God raised from the dead, by Him this man stands here before you whole" (Acts 4:10). Matchless name! The secret of power was in it. When they used the name power struck. The dynamite of heaven exploded.

Peter and John were hustled to jail. The church in Jerusalem prayed for them in "the name." They were released. They went to the church. The entire church prayed that signs and wonders might be done. How did they pray? In "the name." They used it legally. The vital response was instantaneous. The place was shaken as by an earthquake. Tremendous name!'

Jesus commanded: "Go and teach all nations" What for? To proclaim the name. To use the name. To baptize believers. How? In the name. Amazing name. In it was concentrated the combined authority resident in the Father, the Son, and the Holy Spirit. Almighty name!

The apostles used the name. It worked. The deacons at Samaria used the name. The fire flashed. Believers everywhere, forever, were commanded to use it. The name detonated around the World.

More Bibles are sold today than any other 100 books. Why? The name is in it. It's finality—at the name of Jesus every knee shall bow and every tongue confess!"

Prayer in this name gets answers. The Moravians prayed—the greatest revival till that time hit the world. Finney prayed—America rocked with the power. Hudson Taylor prayed—China's Inland Mission was born. Evan Roberts prayed seven years—the Welsh revival resulted.

Before the world-wide revival at the Azusa Street Mission, old Tom Seymour prayed five hours a day for three and one-half years. He prayed seven hours a day for two and one-half years more. Heaven's fire fell over the world, and the most extensive revival of real religion in this century resulted. All because of the name of Jesus.

Filling and Control by the Holy Spirit

The filling or control of the Holy Spirit at times in the work of the kingdom of God is crucial for those things that God *needs* to have done, for He cannot leave essential works to our puny ability to hear and obey Him—and to our often weak faith. That should be easy to understand. So His solution is simple. To those who are devoting themselves to learning His ways, abiding in His word, and walking in His Spirit, He at times fills them with the Holy Spirit and imparts to them the faith and power they need to do what He wants done—and to protect them when they need protection.

It is written about Moses and the Israelites that Moses knew God's ways, the Israelites knew God's acts—many of them performed by Moses. How did that come about? God made it so. "*He made known His ways to Moses, His acts to the children of Israel"* (Psalm 103:7). And He made it so because Moses obeyed Him and the Israelites did not.

If like Moses we would know God's ways, we would not only see far more of God's acts in healing and delivering sick people, we would also at times perform mighty works of power in the name of Jesus Christ as God determined by His Holy Spirit.

Miracles — Works of Power

What is a miracle? It is the tangible evidence of the supreme control of the Spirit of God over every character and form of materiality.

Beloved, the power of such an event, such an act and sign, shows you that through living, positive, contact with the Spirit of God, all things are possible. Blessed be His name!

Christianity is the divine power of Jesus Christ by the Holy Spirit, filling a Christian's soul and body, flashing through his nature like a holy flame, accomplishing the will of God.

There is a baptism that belongs to Jesus Christ. It is in His supreme control. No angel or human can bestow it. It comes from Him alone.

He it is "who baptizes with the Holy Spirit" (John 1:33). So the individual who wants the Holy Spirit must come into definite, conscious, contact with Jesus Christ Himself. Bless God!

I was away from the city of Spokane for a while, and the day I returned Mrs. Lake wasn't at home. I was about to leave for my afternoon service when someone came in and said, "Your secretary, Mrs. Graham, is dying. Your wife is with her."

Immediately I hurried to the place. One of my ministers' wives met me at the door and said, "You're too late, she's gone."

As I stepped inside, the minister was coming out of the room. He said, "She hasn't breathed for a long time."

But looking on that woman, I thought of how God Almighty had raised her out of death three years before, how He had miraculously given her back her womb, ovaries, and tubes that had been removed, and how she had married and conceived a child.

As these thoughts arose, my heart flamed!

I took that woman up off the pillow and called on God for the lightnings of heaven to blast the power of death and deliver her. I commanded her to come back and stay. She came back after having not breathed for twenty-three minutes!

Beloved, we have not yet learned to keep in living touch with the powers of God. Once in awhile our souls rise, and we see the flame of God accomplish this wonder and that. But Jesus Christ lived in the presence of God every hour of the day and night. Not a word came from the mouth of Jesus Christ that was not God's Word. He said, "The words that I speak to you are spirit, and they are life" (John 6:63).

When you and I are lost in the Son of God and the fires of Jesus Christ burn in our hearts, as they did in His, our words will be the words of Spirit and of life. There will be no death in them. Beloved, we are on the way.

The Filling and Ministry of the Holy Spirit

You see, the spirit of man must contact and know the real Spirit of God—know God. We do not know God with our flesh, with our hands, or with our brains. We know God with our spirit. The knowledge of God that our spirit acquires may be conveyed to us through the medium of our mind. The effect of God in our body comes through the medium of our spirit, through our soul, and into our body.

There is a quickening by the Spirit of God so that our body, our soul, and our spirit all alike become blessed, pervaded, and filled with the presence of God Himself in us. The Word of God is wonderfully clear along these lines. For instance, the Word of God says, "You will keep him in perfect peace, Whose mind is stayed on You, Because he trusts in You" (Isaiah 26:3). Why? "Because He trusts in You." That is the peace a Christian knows whose mind rests in God in real perfect trust. "You will keep him in perfect peace, Whose mind is stayed on You."

The Word of God again says that our flesh will rejoice; not our mind but our very flesh will rejoice. The presence of God is to be a living presence, not only in our spirit, nor in our mind alone, but also in our very flesh—so that God is known in all the areas of our life. We know God in our very flesh, we know God in our mind, we know God in our spirit. Bless His precious name!

The medium by which God undertakes to bless the world is through the transmission of Himself. Now the Spirit of God is His own substance, the substance of His being—the very nature and quality of the presence of the nature and being of God. Consequently, when we speak of the Spirit of God being transmitted to us and into us, we are not talking about an influence, either spiritual or mental. We are talking about the transmission of the living substance and being of God into your being and into mine. Not a mental effect, but a living substance. The living being and actual life transmitted, imparted, coming from God into your being, into my being. Bless God!

That is the secret of the abundant life of which Jesus spoke. Jesus said, "I have come that they may have life, and that they may have it more abundantly" (John 10:10). The reason we have the more abundant life is that as we receive God into our being, all the springs of our being are quickened by His living presence. Consequently, when we receive God—via His Holy Spirit—we live life in a fuller measure. We live life with a greater energy, because we become the recipients of the energy of the living God in addition to our normal energy, through the reception of His being, His nature, His life into ours.

Lake's Progression into the Fullness of the Holy Spirit

I knelt under a tree when about sixteen years of age, in repentance and prayer, and God came into my soul. I was saved from my sins and from that day I knew Jesus Christ as a living Savior. There never was a single moment of question about the reality of His incoming into my life as a Savior, for He saved me from my sins. My friend said, "You are baptized in the Holy Ghost."

Sanctified

Sometime later, I think when I was yet under twenty or thereabouts, I met a Christian farmer, Melvin Pratt, who sat down on his plow handles and taught me the subject of sanctification, and God let me enter into that experience. My friends said, "Now surely you are baptized in the Holy Ghost."

Later in my life, I came under the ministry of George B. Watson, of the Christian & Missionary Alliance, who taught with more clearness and better distinction between the baptism of the Holy Ghost and sanctification, and I entered into a richer life and a better experience. A beautiful anointing of the Spirit was upon my life.

Ministry of Healing

Then the ministry of healing was opened to me, and I ministered for ten years in the power of God. Hundreds and hundreds of people were healed by the power of God during this ten years, and I could feel the conscious flow of the Holy Spirit through my soul and my hands.

But at the end of that year, I believe I was the hungriest man for God that ever lived. There was such a hunger for God that as I left my offices in Chicago and walked down the street, my soul would break out, and I would cry, "Oh God!" I have had people stop and look at me in wonder. It was the yearning passion of my soul, asking for God in a greater measure than I then knew. But my friends would say, "Mr. Lake, you have a beautiful baptism in the Holy Ghost." Yes, it was nice as far as it went, but it was not answering the cry of my heart. I was growing up into a large understanding of God and my own soul's need. My soul was demanding a greater entrance into God, His love, presence, and power.

My Baptism in the Holy Spirit

Then one day an old man strolled into my office, sat down, and in the next half hour he revealed more of the knowledge of God to my soul than I had ever known before. When he left I said, "God bless that old gray head. That man knows more of God than any man I ever met. By the grace of God, if that is what the baptism of the Holy Ghost does, I am going to possess it." Oh, the wonder of God that was then revealed to my heart!

I went into fasting and prayer and waiting on God for nine months. Then one day the glory of God in a new manifestation and a new incoming came to my life. And when the phenomena had passed, and the glory of it remained in my soul, I found that my life began to manifest in the varied range of the gifts of the Spirit, . . . and God flowed through me with a new force. Healings were of a more powerful order. Oh, God lived in me; God manifested in me; God spoke through me. My spirit was deified, and I had a new comprehension of God's will, new discernment of spirit, a new revelation of God in me.

A Body Filled and Flooded with God

When God's nature and very being flows into us by the Holy Spirit, we are in essence experiencing the answer to Paul's prayers for all the saints in his letter to the church at Ephesus.

> *For this reason I bow my knees to the Father of our Lord Jesus Christ, from whom the whole family in heaven and earth is named, that He would grant you, according to the riches of His glory, to be strengthened with might through His Spirit in the inner man, that Christ may dwell in your hearts through faith; that you, being rooted and grounded in love, may be able to comprehend with all the saints what is the width and length and depth and height; to know the love of Christ which passes knowledge; that you may be filled with all the fullness of God* (Ephesians 3:14-19).

Or as the Amplified Bible so marvelously translates verse 19:

> *[That you may really come] to know — practically, through experience for yourselves—the love of Christ, which far surpasses mere knowledge (without experience); that you may be filled (through all your being) unto all the fullness of God—[that is] may have the richest measure of the*

divine Presence, and become a body wholly filled and flooded with God Himself!

Faith, the Holy Spirit, and power flowing from God through Jesus Christ to you — and from you to the sick and oppressed.

SEVEN

Be Holy and Righteous

*Do you not know that you are the temple of God and that
the Spirit of God dwells in you? . . . the temple of God is
holy, which temple you are* (1 Corinthians 3:16, 17b).

*The effective, fervent prayer of a righteous man avails
much. Elijah was a man with a nature like ours, and he
prayed earnestly that it would not rain; and it did not rain
on the land for three years and six months. And he prayed
again, and the heaven gave rain, and the earth produced
its fruit* (James 5:16-18).

Holiness has to do with the condition of the heart,
righteousness has to do with right actions and a right
standing with God. Holiness is birthed out of
sanctification—separateness from the world, and
righteousness is birthed out of holiness.

Because God is holy, Jesus Christ is holy, the Holy Spirit
is holy, the Scriptures tell us that we should also be holy, or
we shall not see the Lord. And we are to not only desire
holiness but also to pursue it—run after it until we catch it.

*Pursue . . . holiness, without which no one will
see the Lord* (Hebrews 12:14).

He who called you is holy, you also be holy in all your conduct, because it is written, "Be holy, for I am holy (1 Peter 1:15-16).

Yet many today seem to believe that they can draw a continual stream of power from God without being holy in their spirit, soul, and body, and righteous in their actions. But it has never been so. Throughout the long history of the Church, and back through the dark years to creation, the degree of power flowing from God through one of His children has always been directly related to the degree of that person's holiness and righteousness. It has always been so and always will be so. God's unchanging holy nature requires it.

" ... you are the temple of the living God. As God has said: "I will dwell in them And walk among them. I will be their God, And they shall be My people." Therefore "Come out from among them And be separate, says the Lord. Do not touch what is unclean, And I will receive you." I will be a Father to you, And you shall be My sons and daughters, Says the LORD Almighty." Therefore, having these promises, beloved, let us cleanse ourselves from all filthiness of the flesh and spirit, perfecting holiness in the fear of God (2 Corinthians 6:16-7:1).

Pure Water of the Holy Spirit

In the world today there is not much pure water left. So because of the growing pollution of our water, it is increasingly recommended that every house have filters to remove the impurities and contaminants from the drinking water. That we drink only purified water for the sake of our physical health, and some say even our mental health.

Why should we think, in this age of growing immoral pollution, that anything less is required for our spiritual health? If we want the purity and full force of the water of life to flow through us to others—and for ourselves—then we must use all the spiritual filters God has provided to protect and cleanse us from the storm surge of moral pollution that every day tries to flood our spirits, souls, and bodies. The pure water of the Holy Spirit promised to us by Jesus cannot flow in full force and purity through clogged unclean pipes.

He who believes in Me, as the Scripture has said, out of his heart will flow rivers of living water." But this He spoke concerning the Spirit, whom those believing in Him would receive (John 7:38-39a).

Think of it. If God's children are holy and righteous in spirit, soul, and body, the full force of the pure water of life—the Holy Spirit—will flow through them to bring salvation and healing to hundreds and thousands. It would be as the waters of Ezekiel 47 and Revelation 22 flowing through Christians for the healing of many in many nations.

Granted, it is all a matter of degrees, and no Christian in this morally polluted world can be 100 percent free of its contaminants. So the full force of the Holy Spirit will never be able to flow pure and unimpeded as He did through Jesus—except for those times when He controls us fully for God's own purpose. As demonstrated at times through Tom Seymour at the old Azusa Street Mission in California.

Lake on God in Us

I was in a meeting in Los Angeles on one occasion. Old Tom Seymour was conducting the services and he had the funniest vocabulary that any man ever had. But

I want to tell you there were doctors and lawyers and professors listening to marvelous things coming from the old man's lips. It was not what he said in words, but it was what he said from his spirit to my heart that showed me he had more of God in his life than any man I had ever met up to that time. It was God in him that was attracting people.

There was one man who insisted on getting up and talking every little while. Some people have a mania for talking. Every once in awhile he would get up—and Tom had endured it for a long time. Presently, he got up again, and the old man stuck his finger out and said, "In the name of Jesus Christ sit down." He did not sit down—he fell down as if shot and his friends carried him out.

That is only one manifestation of the living fact of what real Christianity is: *The divine power of Jesus Christ, by the Holy Ghost, filling our soul and body and flashing through our nature like a holy flame, accomplishing the will of God.*

That we may be the temple of the Holy Ghost brings a demand on our consciousness that nothing else in the world can bring. If God has ordained that our spirit, soul, and body may become the living, conscious, temple of His Spirit—that He, God, by His Spirit will live in us and manifest Himself through us, what kind of demand does that bring upon us?

We can understand then, what was in the mind of the Apostle when he said, "What manner of persons ought you to be in holy conduct and godliness?" (2 Peter 3:11).

Why is it that people are slow to yield themselves to the control and government and guidance of the Spirit of God? Why is it that there is not a divine passion in our hearts that such a blessed control should be made a possibility? Shall you and I today assert our own little humanity, and walk according to our own light? Or shall we do as the wise men and women of old did, do as those who seek the divinest in life, and say "Yes" to God and let God take our being—inhabit our spirit, soul, and body, and live His life in us? If we do and He so consents, then we will manifest His life through us!

God's Holy Mountain

No matter where we are at this moment, no matter what our present level of spiritual power, no matter how strong our current contact with the dynamic energy of God, there is a mountain we can climb to the throne of God. Each day, through dedication and determination, holiness and righteousness, we can climb higher than we did the day before—for our sake and the sake of the sick and oppressed.

> *Who may ascend into the hill of the LORD? Or who may stand in His holy place? He who has clean hands and a pure heart, Who has not lifted up his soul to an idol, Nor sworn deceitfully. He shall receive blessing from the LORD, And righteousness from the God of his salvation* (Psalm 24:3-5).

> *Therefore, having these promises, beloved, let us cleanse ourselves from all filthiness of the flesh and spirit, perfecting holiness in the fear of God* (2 Corinthians 7:1).

Holiness to the Lord

Holiness is the character of God. The very substance of His being and essence of His nature is purity. The purpose of God in the salvation of humanity is to produce in human beings a similar holiness, a radiant purity like that of God Himself. If God were unable to produce in us such a purity, then His purpose for us would be a failure, and the object of the sacrifice of Jesus Christ would be a miscarriage instead of a triumph.

The triumph of Jesus Christ was attained through His willingness to be led by the Spirit of God. The triumph of the Christian can be attained only in a similar manner. Even though God has baptized you with the Holy Spirit, there yet remains, as with Jesus, the necessity of walking in humility and permitting the Spirit of God to be your absolute guide.

The unveiling of consciousness, of the desire of the flesh, of the sensuality of the nature and the thoughts, the revelation of adverse tendencies, is part of God's purpose and necessary for growth in God. How can the nature of a person be changed except that nature is first revealed? So there arises in your heart the desire and prayer for the Spirit of God to eject, crucify, and destroy every tendency of opposition to the Holy Spirit. Do not think that you will attain the highest in God until within your own soul there is a heavenly longing to be like Him who gave His life for us.

Do not think to come within the court of God with stain upon your garments. Do not think that heaven can smile upon a nature fouled through evil contact. Do not think that Christ can dwell in temples seared by flames of hate. No! The heart must first be purged by holy fire and washed from every stain by cleansing blood.

" ... *the blood of Jesus Christ His Son [continually] cleanses us from all sin*" (1 John 1:7b).

Do you not know that those whose nature is akin to God's must ever feel the purging power of Christ within?

If you would understand the ways of God, you must trust the Spirit's power to guide and keep. If you would tread the paths where angels tread, you must realize angelic purity. That's the nature of God, that's the working of the Spirit's power, that's what you must attain to overcome. When you do, the joy and power of God will be yours. Healing streams of life will flow through you, and Heaven's gates will open wide. In you the kingdom of God will be revealed.

"And heal the sick there, and say to them, 'The kingdom of God has come near to you'" (Luke 10:9).

Christians live in the light. Christians live in the glory. Christians live in the power of God, in the eternal presence of God. And it is that consciousness of God and union with Him that gives you strength and assurance and confidence and helps you to go on your way regardless of conditions and circumstances, so that you are not being governed by this thing or that, but by the faith of God. Instead of conditions controlling you, you are controlling conditions. That is the power of God.

Living in the High and Holy Place of Spiritual Power

God is endeavoring by His Spirit in these days to lift the souls of Christians into a high place, a holy life, a heavenly state where they walk day by day and hour by hour in the heavenly consciousness of the presence of Christ.

The presence of Christ in the souls of Christians can only produce the purity that is in Him. Purity is of God. Purity is of the nature of Christ. Purity is heaven's atmosphere, filling your soul and making you in your nature like the Son of God. Upon your purified soul there comes from God that blessed measure of the Holy Spirit, not only purifying your nature, but empowering you by the Spirit so that the activities of God, the gift of His mind, the power of His Spirit is evident by the grace of God in your soul and your life.

This will lift you by the grace of God into that place of holy and heavenly dominion in the consciousness of which Jesus lived and moved and accomplished the will of God. Not the earth-consciousness, born of the earth and earthy. The heaven-consciousness, that high consciousness, that holy consciousness, the consciousness of the living God, of His union with Him, that caused Jesus to walk as a conqueror on the earth.

Creative Power of God

Jesus was not bowed and overcome by conditions and circumstances about Him. He knew that the soul was a creative power, that it was the nature of every person to protect, accumulate, and possess as children of God, and that through the creative faculty of your soul the desires of your heart might be brought to pass.

That is the reason God spoke to Moses as He did. That is the reason God rebuked Moses when he stopped to pray. That is the reason God said, "Why do you cry to Me? Tell the children of Israel to go forward. ... lift up your rod, and stretch out your hand over the sea and divide it. And the children of Israel shall go on dry ground through the midst of the sea."

Beloved, your soul will never demonstrate the power of God in any appreciable degree until your soul conceives and understands the real vision of Christ. He knew that through His union with the living God His soul became the creative power through which He took possession of the power of God and applied it to the needs of His own soul and the needs of other lives.

"I am the resurrection and the life," He said to Martha. Lazarus was dead. The friends were weeping, but the Son of God was there. Opening His soul to God in a cry of prayer, the Spirit of God so moved within Him that the consciousness of His high dominion in God so possessed Him, that He gave forth that wondrous command, "Lazarus, come forth!" The dead Lazarus obeyed the call, and his spirit that had gone on into the regions of the dead returned, was rejoined to his body, and Lazarus was restored by the power of God. (John 11:25-44)

The Place of Victory

So much of the difficulty with us all is that we have come down out of the heavenlies into the natural, and we are trying to live a heavenly life in the natural state, overburdened by the weights and cares of the flesh and life all about us. There is deliverance. There is victory. There is a place in God where our flesh is no longer in bondage. A place where by the grace of God every sensuous state of the human nature is brought into subjection to the living God. A place where Christ reigns in and glorifies the very activities of your nature, making you sweet, pure, and clean—good and true.

I call on you today, beloved, by the grace of God, to that high life, to that holy walk, to that heavenly atmosphere, to that life in God where the grace and Spirit and power of God permeate your whole being. When it does, not only your whole being will be in subjection, but power will flow from your nature as a holy stream of heavenly life to bless other souls everywhere by the grace of God—truly bringing to them the kingdom of God.

There was a period in my life when God lifted my soul to a wondrous place of divine power. Indeed, I say with all humility that I believe God gave me an anointing of power that has seldom been manifested in modern life. That anointing remained with me for a period of eight months. One of the evidences of the power of God at that period was that God gave me such a consciousness of dominion to cast out evil spirits that the insane were brought to me from all parts of the land.

Often as I approached them, the Spirit of Christ would rise up in me in such dominion that when I got to them I could take hold of them, and looking into their face, would realize that God had given me power to cast out the evil spirit. Hundreds of times the insane were healed instantly, right where they stood.

I have been a student all my life—not just a student of letters, but of the things of the soul. By God's grace, I noted that when that high consciousness of heavenly dominion rested upon my life, there was one thing that stood uppermost in all my consciousness. That was the vision of the triumphant Christ, the Son of God, as pictured by John in the first chapter of Revelation, where He stands forth in the mighty dignity of an overcomer and declared, "I am He who lives, and was dead, and behold, I am alive forevermore. Amen. And I have the keys of Hades and of Death" (Revelation 1:18).

The soul joined to Christ, exercising the power of God, ascends into the high consciousness of heavenly dominion as it is in the heart of Jesus Christ today, for He is the overcomer, the only overcomer. But when your soul is joined to His soul, when His Spirit flows like a heavenly stream through your spirit, when your whole nature is infilled and inspired by the life from God, you also become an overcomer in deed and in truth—because you are joined to Christ.

I am glad that God has permitted us to rise into that place of high dominion in Christ even at intervals, for it demonstrates the purpose of God. It demonstrates that He purposes we should not only rise into the high place at intervals, but that this should be the normal life of the Christian who is joined to Christ.

Christianity does not need to be apologized for. Christianity is the living, conscious, life and power of the living God, transmitted into the nature of a human being until the person's nature is transformed by the living touch. The spirit, soul, and body is energized and filled by His life. Thus, you become as God intended, a form of Christ.

Ultimate Goal of the Gospel

That startles some people. But the ultimate goal of the Gospel of Jesus Christ, and the ultimate goal of the redemption of the Son of God, is to reproduce and make every person who is bound by sin and held by sensuousness and enslaved by the flesh, like Himself in deed and in truth—sons of God. Not sons of God on a lower order, but sons of God as Jesus was.

Paul declares, "He Himself gave some to be apostles, some prophets, some evangelists, and some pastors and teachers." For what purpose? " ... till we all come to ... a perfect man, to the measure of the stature of the fullness of Christ" (Ephesians 4:11, 13).

Not a limited life, but an unlimited life. The idea of God was that every person should be transformed into Christ's perfect image through being joined to Him by the Holy Spirit. Christ within and Christ without. Christ in your spirit, Christ in your soul, and Christ in your body. Not only living His life, but performing His works by the grace of God. That is the Gospel of the Son of God. That is the thing that Paul was not ashamed of. He said, "I am not ashamed of the gospel of Christ, for it is the power of God to salvation for everyone who believes, for the Jew first and also for the Greek" (Romans 1:16).

The holy life of Christ pouring through Paul and the other apostles and early Christians gave them not only spiritual power, but also a boldness and courage that enabled them to turn their world upside down, It could be the same today.

These who have turned the world upside down have come here too (Acts 17:6b).

EIGHT

Be Bold and Courageous

*Now, Lord, look on their threats, and grant to Your
servants that with all boldness they may speak Your word,
by stretching out Your hand to heal, and that signs and
wonders may be done through the name of Your holy
Servant Jesus." And when they had prayed, the place
where they were assembled together was shaken; and they
were all filled with the Holy Spirit, and they spoke the
word of God with boldness (Acts 4:29-31).*

*Be strong and of good courage, . . . Only be strong and
very courageous, . . . Be strong and of good courage; do
not be afraid, nor be dismayed, for the LORD your God
is with you wherever you go (Joshua 1:6-7, 9).*

They spoke the Word of God with boldness." What
marvelous words those are! "They spoke the Word of
God with boldness." In these days of uncertainty and
timidity about the Word of God, and the preaching of many
things that are purported to be the Word of God but are
not, those words have a clarity and strength about them
that are well needed today.

When God told Joshua to do in three days what Moses
had not been able to do—to take His people into the
Promised Land, He three times urged and encouraged him

to be strong and courageous. And from the moment you are reading this, back down through the grand history of the Church and God's redemptive work with His chosen people, it has always been strong and courageous leaders, those bold in the Word of God, who have taken God's people into the purposes and promises of God.

What enabled them to be that way, to be bold, strong, and courageous in the true Word of God? An absolute conviction that the same source of strength and courage that was with Joshua was with them. " … for the LORD your God is with you wherever you go." The spiritual principle established throughout the Bible is simple: If God sends you somewhere, you never go alone; if He tells you to do something, you never do it alone—God is *always* with you.

> *All authority has been given to Me in heaven and on earth. Go therefore and make disciples of all the nations, baptizing them in the name of the Father and of the Son and of the Holy Spirit, teaching them to observe all things that I have commanded you; and lo, I am with you always, even to the end of the age* (Matthew 28:18b-20).

> *And I will pray the Father, and He will give you another Helper, that He may abide with you forever; the Spirit of truth, whom the world cannot receive, because it neither sees Him nor knows Him; but you know Him, for He dwells with you and will be in you. I will not leave you orphans; I will come to you* (John 14:16-18).

So knowing the history of how God works with His people, and facing threats of punishment for speaking and teaching in the name of Jesus, the disciples prayed, *"Grant to Your servants that with all boldness they may speak Your word,* by *stretching out Your hand to heal, and that signs and wonders may be done through the name of Your holy Servant Jesus."* Do signs and wonders through the very name that we have been commanded not to speak or teach about (Acts 4:18). Give a visible sign to all that You are with us when we speak that name, and that will enable us to speak Your Word with boldness.

> *And when they had prayed, the place where they were assembled together was shaken; and they were all filled with the Holy Spirit, and they spoke the word of God with boldness ... And with great power the apostles gave witness to the resurrection of the Lord Jesus. And great grace was upon them all* (Acts 4:31, 33).

Signs and wonders will enable you to speak the true and pure Word of God with boldness and courage almost more than anything else will. In fact, when God begins to do signs and wonders through you in the name of Jesus Christ, you won't want to speak or hear anything other than the true and pure Word of God. Everything else that is being preached and taught today will seem to you like another Jesus and a different gospel (2 Corinthians 11:4). And you will find yourself standing on such a sure and certain foundation that you cannot be moved from it (1 Corinthians 3:11) As Smith Wigglesworth said, "The person who has an experience is never at the mercy of a person who has only an argument."

Now in Joshua's case, all visible signs of the presence of God disappeared shortly after the Israelites entered the Promised Land. There was no more cloud by day and night, and the manna ceased on the day after they had eaten the produce of the land (Joshua 5:12).

Soon they would start their first of many battles against the enemies of God in the Promised Land, but first there was the appearance of the Man with the sword in His hand, the "Commander of the army of the LORD" (Joshua 5:13-15).

When Joshua saw Him, he went up to Him and asked, "Are You for us or for our adversaries?"

To which the Man replied, "No."

A strange answer, and not an answer at all to Joshua's question. But in the Man's answer of "No," there was a deeper statement. It was this: "I have not come to be for you or for your adversaries, I have come to take over." And surely we understand that the appearance of the "Commander of the army of the LORD" was an epiphany, a pre-gospel appearance of Christ, a manifestation intended to reveal something of great spiritual importance to us.

Understanding that, we should realize that when we receive Jesus as our Lord and Savior, the Spirit of Christ comes into us by the Holy Spirit, not to be for or against us, but to take over. Thus He is always with us—as our Savior, yes, but more importantly as our Lord. Knowing that should enable us to be strong and courageous in the things of God in the same way that He urged Joshua to be—and for the same reason.

When you realize that Christ is always with you and speak the Word of God with boldness and courage, you will find yourself acting that way in all your endeavors for God.

Shoulders Healed of Rheumatism

One Saturday night in South Africa the church was packed. There was not even any standing room left. I was preaching on the power of God and in a strong spirit was endeavoring to demonstrate that Jesus Christ is the same yesterday, today, and forever. To state boldly that His power is as great as it ever was, and that the only qualification for touching God for anything is faith in Him. The audience was greatly moved.

As I continued preaching, I saw a gentleman and two ladies trying to squeeze through the people who were standing in the aisles. I asked the crowd to separate and permit the ladies to come through. I tried to arrange seating space for them on the steps of the platform.

As they approached, I noticed that one of the ladies held her arms perfectly stiff. She did not move them at all. I seemed to know at once that she was suffering from rheumatism.

When she got to the platform, I asked, "What is the reason you don't move your arms?"

She said. "My shoulders are set from rheumatism."

I said, "How long have they been like this?"

She replied, "Ten years."

I asked if she had been treated by physicians.

She replied, "I have been discharged from three hospitals as incurable."

"What hospitals?"

She answered, "Kimberley, Johannesburg, and Pretoria."

I asked the gentleman who accompanied her, "Do you know this lady?"

He said, "Yes, she is my sister-in-law."

I said, "Do you know her story to be correct?"

"Absolutely," he said.

I asked her what she had come for.

She replied, "In the hope that the Lord would heal me."

I asked, "Do you want me to pray for you for healing?"

"Yes," she said.

The crowd in the aisles and around the doors was noisy, and I spoke directly to them. "You people never saw Jesus heal a person in your life. You do not know anything about this matter. You have never witnessed an exhibition of the power of God, and therefore you should be considerate enough to keep still, confess your ignorance of such matters, and learn.

"This is what I want: Select two men from your group, and let then come and see for themselves if this woman's arms are stiff as she says."

I waited for them to make their selection. Two men came forward, examined the lady's arms critically, and found them to be as she had said—quite immovable.

I asked the men, "Have you finished your examination? Are you satisfied her condition is as stated?"

They said, "We are."

"Then stand back, for I am going to pray that the Lord will heal this woman."

Placing my hands on the woman's shoulders, I commanded in the name of Jesus Christ, the Son of God, that the rheumatic devil that bound the woman leave her. In Christ's name, I commanded it to go, rebuking it with all the energy of my soul. The power of God flashed through me like a burning fire until perspiration burst from the woman's face.

I then took her by the hands and said, "In the name of Jesus Christ, put your arms up!"

The right arm went up.

I said, "In the name of Jesus Christ put the other arm up, too."

She instantly obeyed. Both arms had become free!

Delighted at being healed, the woman held both arms up, praising God, and headed for the door. The crowd parted for her, and she disappeared. I did not see her again for some months. When I did see her again, she was still healed.

Epileptic Seizure

Once after an inspired address almost the whole congregation moved forward to the penitent form, when a big man fell near the front in an epileptic seizure. Like a flash, Lake was off the platform, and at his side, rebuking the demon in the name of Jesus, and then he quietly returned to the platform. But the work was done. The fit was cut short, and the man never had another.

Hypnotic Spirit Cast Out

About a year ago at a Sunday service in our Johannesburg Tabernacle, God instantly healed a lame girl. She came from Germiston [in Gauteng, NE South Africa]. She had been suffering for three and a half years from what doctors said was either an extreme case of rheumatism or the first stage of hip disease. She was not able to get up the steps without assistance, when she came to the platform to be prayed for.

One of our ministers asked her, "How long have you been sick?"

She said, "For three and a half years."

"Have doctors treated you?"

"Yes, for two and a half years, but they haven't been able to help me."

"Who has been treating you for the last year?"

"A hypnotist."

Just then a well-known hypnotist arose in the audience, moved forward and took a front seat, apparently so he could see better. The minister said, "Never mind the hypnotist. Jesus is going to heal you right now. In two minutes you will be well."

Several laid hands on her and prayed, and instantly the Lord delivered her, and she walked up and down the platform several times to demonstrate to herself and the audience that she was well.

I stood back and looked at her, my heart going out in praise to God for His mercy. Then suddenly the Spirit of the Lord descended upon me in power, not in any gentle influence, but with a mighty intense power, a spirit of revulsion against the spirit of the hypnotist. I went to the edge of the platform directly in front of him and said, "Are you the man who has been hypnotizing this woman?"

He replied, "Yes, I am." He rose to his feet and looked at me as if challenging me.

I said to him, "In the Name of Jesus Christ, you will never hypnotize anybody again." *And before I realized what I was doing,* I reached over the front of the platform, grasped his collar with my left hand, while with my right I slapped him on the back, saying, "In the Name of Jesus Christ, the Son of God, you come out of him."

He laughed at me and said, "Do you mean to tell me that I cannot hypnotize anybody?"

I said, "Yes, sir, that is the end of that thing. The devil that caused you to hypnotize people is out."

He worked all night trying to hypnotize some subjects, and in the morning at six came to my house saying, "This is a mighty serious business, mister, this is my bread and butter. I'll give you a large sum of money if you'll give me back my power to hypnotize."

I said, "Man, I didn't take it away from you, it was Jesus who cast out the devil. Thank Him that you're rid of it. You'll never hypnotize another person as long as you live, so go earn an honest living. It looks to me like that's what the Lord wants from you."

He cancelled his engagement at the theater where he was billed to give exhibitions, and the last we heard, he was working in a mine and earning an honest living. That demonstrated that there is a mighty manifestation of the Spirit of God that has dominion over every other power. It is still true that in Jesus' name we shall cast out devils.

Have Faith and Boldness

It takes faith and boldness to exercise your gift from God. There are just lots of people around everywhere who have gifts from God and they are lying dormant in their lives. So there is no value for the kingdom of God through them because of the fact that they have no faith in God to boldly exercise the gift and get the benefit of it.

Timothy probably was a timid fellow, and Paul had to show him why he should be exercising the gift from God that he believed to be in him.

For God has not given us a spirit of fear (2 Timothy 1:7).

I confess I would like to swear sometimes at preachers who are all the time preaching fear. They preach fear of the devil and fear of demons and fear of this influence and fear of that influence and fear of some other power. If the Holy Spirit has come from heaven into your soul, common sense teaches us that by so doing He has made you the master of every other power in the world—otherwise the Word of God is a blank falsehood, for Jesus Himself declared:

He who is in you is greater than he who is in the world (1 John 4:4).

Behold, I give you the authority to trample on serpents and scorpions, and over all the power of the enemy, and nothing shall by any means hurt you (Luke 10:19).

If we had faith to believe that "He who is greater" is in us, we would be stepping out with boldness and majesty. The conscious supremacy of the Son of God would be manifest in our lives, and instead of being subservient and bowed down and broken beneath the weight of sin and the powers of darkness around us, they would flee from us and keep out of our way. I believe before God that there is not a devil that comes within a hundred feet of a real God-anointed Christian. That is the kind of vision God put in my soul.

Witch Doctors

When I went to South Africa years ago, I attended a great missionary conference a short time after I was there. It was a general conference of the Christian missions of the country. On account of our teaching the baptism of the Holy Spirit and the power of God to heal, we were a peculiar people in the conference. We were bringing a new message and they wanted to hear us and size us up and classify us.

Among the problems they discussed in that conference, was the tremendous influence of the native witch doctors over the people—their so-called medicine men. They had developed tremendous psychic powers because for generations and generations they studied psychic things until they understood the practice of psychic laws. It is amazing to see the psychic manifestations they bring to pass. I have seen shocking things take place at the hand of witch doctors, things that you would not believe unless you saw them.

On one occasion, two men had become extremely jealous of each other. They were both native chiefs, and they lived sixty miles from each other One time as I was in the village of one of them, I heard them discussing a particular problem with the other chief, and it was decided by the village chief that the next Sunday morning he was going to set the other fellow on fire. I wanted to see this phenomenon, and I got a horse and went across the country to the other village to be there on Sunday morning.

Every Sunday the chiefs go out and round up their cattle and herds, look over their flocks, count them, and see how they're doing. It's a sort of Sunday exercise. I rode along. We had not ridden for more than an hour when I observed this fellow was becoming very hot. Within half an hour, he was absolutely purple.

After awhile he began to complain of terrible pain, and finally he became exhausted, got down and lay on the ground in a state of total exhaustion. I believe the man would have died. I had heard about these sorts of things, but this was taking place under my own eyes.

I saw that unless the man got deliverance he would die. When it got to that point, I said to the other Christians who were with me, "It's time that we prayed." I stepped over and laid my hands on the chief and called on God to destroy that damning psychic power that was destroying the fellow—and God shattered it and the man lived.

I talked to the Conference about this matter. I said, "It is a strange thing to me that after all the years of missions in this land your hands are tied on account of witch doctors. Why don't you go out and cast the devil out of those fellows and get the people delivered from their power?"

But they were too fearful, and all they did was accuse us of casting out demons by Beelzebub, the same way the Pharisees accused Jesus (Matthew 12:24). "Cast the devil out?" their leader said, "He [God] will cast the devil out of you!"

The secret of our work, the reason God gave us one hundred thousand people, the reason we have twelve hundred native preachers in our work in South Africa is because of the fact we believed the Word of God that, *"He who is in you is greater than he who is in the world"* (1 John 4:4).

We not only went to find the witch doctors, but also challenged them separately and together and by the power of God delivered the people from their power. When they were delivered, the people appreciated their deliverance from the slavery in which they had been held through their superstitions and spirit control.

God has not given us a spirit of fear, but of power and of love and of a sound mind (2 Timothy 1:7).

Whenever I got in the presence of one of these fellows and wanted to cast out the devil, I always felt I wanted to look into his eyes. The eyes of a man are the windows of his soul. In teaching a class of children, I asked them what the eyes were for. One little chap said, "Your eyes are for you to look out of."

Do you get it? It is not a poetic expression; they are the windows through which you look out. It is wonderful the things you see when you look out. Sometimes you see fear and the spirit of darkness and you see other life. Marvelous things that you see with your inner eyes. The world laughs at Christian people because they sometimes talk about seeing by the Spirit, but it's now a natural way for us to see.

God Anointed

God anoints your soul. God anoints your life. God comes to dwell in your person. God comes to make you a master over every spiritual power that is not of the Holy Spirit. That is the purpose of His indwelling in a Christian. The real children of God are to be masters over every other power of darkness in the world. It is to be subject to them. They are God's representatives in the world. The Holy Spirit in the Christian is as powerful as the Holy Spirit was in Jesus Christ. Indeed, Jesus goes to such an extreme that He declares:

*"Most assuredly, I say to you, he who believes in Me, the works that I do he will do also; and **greater works than these he will do**, because I go to My Father"* (John 14:12).

This indicates that the mighty Holy Spirit from heaven in the lives of the Christian was to be more powerful in you and in me after Jesus got to heaven and ministered Him to our souls than He was in Jesus.

Faith to Believe

Beloved, who has the faith to believe it? Who has faith to exercise it? We cannot exercise anything beyond what we believe to be possible. Listen: *God has not given us a spirit of fear.*

Fear of the devil is nonsense. Fear of demons is foolish. The Spirit of God anointing the Christian heart makes the soul impregnable to the powers of darkness. How I love to teach that when the Lord Jesus Christ anoints your soul and baptizes you in the Holy Ghost, the almightiness of the eternal God the Father by the Spirit and Jesus Christ combined has come into your soul.

One of the thirty-six articles of the Church of England says, "The Holy Spirit who proceeds from the Father and the Son." There is no truer thing in all the world. Do you get it—"who proceeds from the Father and the Son"?

In the fourth and fifth chapters of Revelation, you see the distinctive personalities of God the Father and Jesus Christ. God the Father occupies the throne and is holding the seven-sealed book in His hand. Jesus Christ, the silent Lamb, without an attendant, not an angel to accompany Him, absolutely alone, in lonesomeness as the slain Lamb, presents Himself to the Father. When He does, the Father hands Him the seven-sealed scroll as the only One who has prevailed and so has the right "to open the scroll and to loose its seven seals" (Revelation 5:5).

Holy Spirit Gives You Power

What I want to bring to you is that the Spirit of God, the divine master, the eternal power of God, the combined life and presence by the Spirit, of the Father and the Son, is given to you. Not to leave you a weakling and subject to all kinds of powers of darkness, but to make you a master, to give you dominion in God over every devilish force that ever was. *God has not given us a spirit of fear, but of power and of love and of a sound mind.*

The Spirit of Power is the Holy Spirit. Not only a Spirit of power, but of love and of a sound mind—not craziness and insanity, but a sound mind by which you can look in the face of the devil and laugh.

Once I was called to come to pray for a blacksmith at Johannesburg, South Africa. He was in delirium tremens. When I got to the house, they had him locked in a room and the windows barred. The wife said, "Mr. Lake, you are not going into that room?"

I said, "Yes, I would like to."

"But, Brother, you do not understand. My sons are all more powerful than you are and four of them tried to overpower him and could not do it. He nearly killed them."

I said, "Dear sister, I have the secret of power that I believe matches this case."

He who is in you is greater than he who is in the world (1 John 4:4).

"Sister, you just give me the key, and go about your work, and do not be troubled." I unlocked the door, slipped into the room, locked the door, and put the key in my pocket. The man was reclining in a crouch like a lion ready to spring. I never heard lips blaspheme as his did. He cursed using every expression I ever heard and worse. He threatened me that if I came near him he would tear me limb from limb and throw me out the window. He was as big as two of me. I never saw such an arm in my life.

I began to talk to him. I had the confidence that "He who is in you is greater than he who is in the world." I engaged him in conversation until the Holy Spirit in me got hold of that devil or a legion as the case might be. I approached the bed step-by-step, sometimes only three inches, and in half an hour, I got up close enough where I could reach his hand. He was still reclining in a posture like a lion. I caught his hand and turned his wrists. I was not practicing any athletic tricks, but I unconsciously turned his wrists over, and as I did it brought my eyes down near his, and all at once I seemed to come awake and be aware of who I was really seeing inside the man.

I could see the devil in that man begin to crawl. He was trying to get away. God Almighty can look out of your eyes, and no demon that exists could look in the eyes of Jesus without crawling. The lightnings of God were there.

My spirit awoke, and I could see the devil in him was in terror and was crawling and trying to get back away from my eyes as far as it could. I looked up to heaven and called on God to cast that devil out and loaned Jesus Christ all the force of my nature, all the power of my spirit, all the power of my mind, and all the power of my body. God had me from the crown of my head to the soles of my feet.

The lightnings of God went through me, and the next thing I knew the man collapsed in a heap and flopped down like a big fish. Then he rolled off the bed onto his knees and began to weep and pray, because the devil was gone from him and he had become human again.

Confidence in God

Dear heart, don't you see in a moment that this character of education develops a certain confidence in God, and it makes your soul sick when you see Christian men and women sneak around afraid of demons and teaching people that some demon is going to jump on you and take possession of you. Not a bit of it! There never was a demon in the world that ever went through the blood of Jesus, if the individual was in Christ.

In the Jewish Bible, among the listings of the covenants, is one that is known as the Threshold Covenant. That was the covenant by which the Israelites went out of the land of Egypt. When God told them to slay a lamb and put the blood on the doorposts and lintel (Exodus 12:7, 22-23). The Jewish Bible adds that they also put the blood on the threshold.

A lot of people get the blood of Jesus on their head, but it seems to me they do not get it under their feet. The Word of God teaches us to get the blood under your feet and on the right hand and on the left hand and over your head. That is your protection. There was no angel of death in the land of Egypt that could go through that blood unto that family. No sir! He was absolutely barred.

Friends, do you believe it was the blood of the Lamb that was barring the angel of death? Do you believe the red stains on the doors frightened him away? No sir, the blood signified to me that there is one that goes through the blood; that is the Holy Ghost. And beloved, the eternal God, by the Spirit, went through the blood to the inside and stayed there and defended the house.

... the one who is in you is greater than the one who is in the world (1 John 4:4 NIV).

All these little insignificant demons that come along in this sickness or that sickness or that temptation of sin have no power over you. Dear friends, from heaven there comes to your heart and mine that dominion of Jesus by which the God-anointed soul walks through them, through myriads of demons, and they cannot touch you.

Christian Have Dominion Over the Devil

I was in Pretoria, South Africa, visiting with a friend and trying to keep out of the hot sun to meditate and pray. As I meditated and prayed, I seemed to be lifted up in the Spirit until I was a mile or more above the city and could see the city like you would from an airplane. When I got up there, I made a discovery. There were myriads of spirits of darkness and myriads of spirits of light in the most awful conflict I ever saw. Naturally, you think of a weapon when you see a fight. I thought, If only I had a weapon I would get into that fight

Presently, the Spirit of God got hold of me, and when these demons came at me from all sides, I waded into them and began to knock them down. It continued until

I had knocked so many down I had to climb over them to get at the rest.

When the vision lifted I prayed, "Dear Lord, what does it mean?"

The Spirit of the Lord said to me, "This battle that you have seen in the upper air will exist among your own people on the earth in six months. This lesson is to teach you that there is a dominion in Jesus Christ, and 'He who is in you is greater than he who is in the world.'"

Friends, it is time you and I as the blood-washed in Jesus awoke to our privilege whereby in the name of the Lord we cease to sin and let no unholy condemnation remain upon our life any longer.

I do not know, but maybe I have come through a different school from what others have in the lines of the Spirit, but I am sure of one thing, that if Christianity was to leave me a weakling to be oppressed by the power of darkness I would seek something else because it would not meet the need. It is that which meets the need that gives you divine supremacy in Jesus Christ. Friend, when your heart is surcharged by that faith in God so that "He who is in you is greater than he who is in the world," you will pray a new prayer.

Moses came to the Red Sea with impassable mountains on the right hand and impassable mountains on the left hand, the army of Pharaoh behind him, and the sea in front of him. If anyone had a right to stop and pray, surely you might say that Moses had.

Over and over and over again, when we get to the real ditch, we try to jump the thing and put the responsibility back on God. Just watch God make a real man. When Moses got his prayer nicely started, God rebuked him and said,

And the LORD said to Moses, "Why do you cry to Me? Tell the children of Israel to go forward. But lift up your rod, and stretch out your hand over the sea and

divide it. And the children of Israel shall go on dry ground through the midst of the sea (Exodus 14:15-16).

I want you to get this. God did not say, "Moses, you stretch out your hand and I will divide the sea." He said, "Stretch out your hand over the sea and *divide* it. You have faith in Me, *you* stretch out your hand and divide the sea."

Jesus said practically the same thing to His disciples:

And when He had called His twelve disciples to Him, He gave them power over unclean spirits, to cast them out, and to heal all kinds of sickness and all kinds of disease (Matthew 10:1). [See also Luke 9:1-6]

Beloved, He gives it to you. What is the Holy Spirit? It is the gift of God Himself to you. The Holy Spirit is not simply given that you may be a channel and always a channel. Absolutely not! The most magnificent thing the Word of God portrays is that Christ indwelling in you by the Holy Spirit is to make you a son of God like Jesus Christ—God-anointed from heaven, with the recognized power of God in your spirit to command the will of God.

It may not be that all souls have grown to that place where such a life as that is evident. But if the Son of God by the Holy Ghost has been born in our hearts, it is time we began to let Him have some degree of sway in our hearts, and some degree of heavenly dominion that has value, and some degree of the lightnings—the flashing streaks of power—of Jesus Christ breaking forth from our spirits.

That is what the Word of God speaks to my soul. That is why my spirit rejoices in this blessed Word.

God has not given us a spirit of fear, but of power and of love and of a sound mind. (2 Timothy 1:7)

The sanest person is the person that believes God and boldly and courageously stands on His promises. That is a person who knows the secret of His power, receives the Holy Spirit, gives Him sway in his life, and goes out in the name of the Lord Jesus to command the will of God and bring it to pass in the world. Unafraid of anything the devil and all his demon forces may bring on.

NINE

Be Unafraid to Fail

"Do not be afraid of their faces, For I am with you to deliver you," says the LORD (Jeremiah 1:8).

"It's not the critic who counts; not the person who points out how the strong person stumbled, or where the doer of deeds could have done better. The credit belongs to those who are actually in the arena; whose faces are marred by dust and sweat and blood; who strive valiantly; who err and come short again and again; who know the great enthusiasms, the great devotions, and spend themselves in a worthy cause; who at the best know in the end the triumph of high achievement; and who at worst, if they fail, at least fail while daring greatly; so that their place shall never be with those cold and timid souls who know neither victory nor defeat." (Theodore Roosevelt)

Failure is the cost of learning to do something right—it is the key to success.

*T*here are millions of Christians who are doing absolutely nothing to get more of God. Then there are those who are studying and praying and forging forward through many spiritual struggles to get the power of God for themselves, for their church, for the sick and the oppressed, and for the glory of God and Christ. Though the latter may not yet have succeeded in obtaining the full power of the Holy Spirit, which of the two groups are the true failures?

As my grandfather used to say, "It doesn't matter how many times you get knocked down, it only matters how many times you get back up. Those who win may have been counted out many times, but they didn't hear the referee."

Christianity needs the Rocky Balboas who will struggle to their feet every time they get knocked down, and though battered, bruised, and bloody, get back into the fight until they win. Christ is in our corner and the Holy Spirit is our trainer—in the end, we cannot fail. Not unless we decide the battle is too difficult and lay down and quit. You are never a failure until you decide to be one.

Fear of Failing

One of the things that hampers those who would minister healing almost more than anything else is fear of failing, being afraid that when they pray for someone to be healed nothing will happen, and so they'll look foolish—or even stupid—to everyone watching them. Those who say that such a thing has never happened to them are kidding themselves. It's a universal problem, and a fear you need to rid yourself of before you can minister effectively.

Fear of failing is the reason that so many who pray for people to be healed put the responsibility for the healing upon the sick person. If the person isn't healed, it isn't their fault, not a failure of their faith; it's the fault of the person for whom they prayed, the person who came to them for prayer. They admonish the unhealed ones to "Just keep believing, brother—just keep believing, sister," and walk heartlessly away, leaving the sick to struggle with their faith, even try to get out of wheelchairs or off stretchers to "put their faith into action."

It's shameful for anyone who takes it upon themselves to minister healing to literally tell people who come to them for prayer that God did not heal them because in their sick and oppressed conditions they did not have enough faith. Thus they save face by putting the responsibility upon the sick and upon God. It should not be so.

John G. Lake never blamed the sick if they were not healed. He believed that all the faith required of the sick was that they ask for prayer and submit to the laying on of hands. That's all the faith Jesus required of them, that's all the faith we should require. It is then the faith of the person or persons praying that heal the sick. This is in keeping with James 5:15—"And the prayer of faith will save the sick, and the Lord will raise him up." It is for that reason and others that Lake encouraged those who weren't healed instantly to continue coming back for more ministry and prayer until they were healed. As Lake says below, "The person who knows God is the one to have faith in God for the healing of others."

John Wesley, the founder of the Methodist church, records two hundred and forty cases of healing as having taken place in his lifetime under his own personal ministry. It included his horse, Dan.

Dan became so lame one time during one of Wesley's preaching trips that he was not able to carry Wesley further. So Wesley got down and prayed by the roadside, and God instantly healed the horse.

I'll guarantee that old Dan did not have any faith. Nobody asked Dan to exercise faith for his healing. The person who knows God is the one to have faith in God.

People say to us these days, "If you have perfect faith, come to me and I will pray and you will be healed."

Say, brothers and sisters, if you have perfect faith you won't need anyone to pray. It is because you do not have perfect faith that Jesus, knowing the imperfection of a human being's faith, made provision for a ministry of divine assistance. "If two of you agree …" (Matthew 18:19).

Why, if I could get along alone, I would never have to have anybody assist me. "If two of you agree…."—so my wife and I agree. We agree in God that this is the will of God and by the grace of God we are going to believe Him, so His will is manifested and it is done.

I agree with the elder or the pastor who comes to minister to me through the prayer of faith. I agree in my spirit with God and with the person who lays hands upon me. If I had perfect faith, I would not need any help.

It is because I am sick, it is because I am down, that I need help from God. And God, knowing all our needs, has made arrangement that you and I shall have the blessing that is necessary and the privilege of the faith of others to lift us out of our darkness and sin.

Fear of People

When God called Jeremiah, he did not want to go. He said it was because he was too young and that he could not speak. But God knew his real problem—it was fear of people, and so He told Jeremiah, "Do not be afraid of their faces, For I am with you to deliver you," says the LORD" (Jeremiah 1:8).

My wife, Beverlee, and I had only been Christians for about two years, but the Lord was already progressively healing her crippling rheumatoid arthritis—the lupus she had was already gone—and in twenty minutes one day I was healed of a slipped disk that I had for over ten years.

We were also beginning to teach in homes, and we were having some success in healing our children of fevers, infections, and pains.

At the time, I worked for a publishing firm, and one of the long-time executives there—we'll call him Aaron—was an agnostic, a science buff, an avid believer in evolution, the most intelligent person I had met to that time, a Jew, and an avid tennis player. We occasionally went out to lunch together.

Late one morning I went into his office to talk to him, and he was flexing his arm and rubbing his right elbow. I asked him what was wrong. "I played a couple of hours of tennis last night, and when I got up this morning my elbow was screaming with pain. For about two months I've been getting it almost every time I play."

We discussed the possibility of "tennis elbow," and he said he was positive that's what it was—and a doctor he went to said the same thing, and he might have to give up tennis, or cut it way back.

All the time we talked I was fighting the worst battle inside that I've ever fought. I was certain that if I prayed for his elbow the pain would go away, but at the same time I was filled with almost a living fear of asking him if I could pray for him in the name of Jesus Christ—both because of what he might say, and because what if I failed? The fear won and I left his office without saying anything about it.

The battle raged within me all afternoon. I knew without any doubt that if I prayed for Aaron the pain would leave, but the fear of going into his office and asking this highly intelligent, agnostic, Jew if I could pray for the healing of his elbow in the name of Jesus Christ was so strong within me that I could not get through it. And in the midst of my certainty that he would be healed, there was fear that he would not be—and what a fool I would look like.

Over and over I pictured myself going into his office, closing the door, and saying, "Aaron, . . ." and that was as far as I could get even within my mind. I finally convinced myself that I would pray all evening that his pain would leave, and would pray that in the morning I would have the boldness and courage to talk to him about praying for his elbow. And so the afternoon ended and we all went home.

When I got to work the next morning, Aaron was already there. I waited about an hour and then went to see him. When I walked into his office, he smiled and flexed his arm three or four times. "Look at this," he said. "My arms fine. I got up this morning and there was no pain, none at all."

After saying some things that I cannot now remember, I went back to my desk. I was stunned, chagrined, humiliated—because inside of me I could literally hear the Lord telling me that he had healed Aaron in answer to my prayers, but that He had not received the glory, and Aaron had not seen the power of the name of Jesus Christ, because I had been afraid of Aaron's face, afraid of failing.

That was over thirty years ago, and only God knows how many times I've thought of that incident and with deep regret wondered about what might have been if only I could have overcome my fears.

Did I get over this "fear of faces?" Yes, slowly . . . with lots of study, prayer, and fasting.

When You Fail

Every person who prays for people to be healed will have more failures than successes. That's just the way it's been in every healing ministry since the days of Jesus. It doesn't matter whose ministry it was—John G. Lake, Smith Wigglesworth, Maria Woodworth Etter, Alexander Dowie, Kathryn Kuhlman, Charles Price, or dozens of others, there were always more failures than successes. If you don't have a lot of failures, it only means you're not praying for a lot of people. But each failure can be a success if you learn from it—and everything you learn will increasingly help you to get more people healed, so your failure rate will keep going down.

Even though you will have failures, you must approach each person as if they are going to be healed instantly—the more you do, the more often they will be. If praying for something like pain, never look at how much pain is still there, look at how much pain is gone, and tell the person for whom you pray to do the same. In other words, even though you will have failures, always look for every degree of success, and build on that.

When you have failures, you will be disappointed, naturally. But never allow yourself to be discouraged. Disappointment and discouragement are two different states of mind. Disappointment can be a stimulus to improvement that will result in success. Discouragement, however, is a mortal enemy that destroys courage and initiative and will rob you of the will to continue to fight for the healing of the sick and oppressed.

Failures do not cause discouragement; your reaction to the failures causes it. So don't give in to it. You cannot escape disappointments, you'll have them many times, it's simply a part of life, and especially a part of ministering to others when you so much want to help them and see them well.

No matter how many times you are disappointed, however, you cannot resign yourself to discouragement, or you will increase your failures and not decrease them. Look at each failure as something that you can learn from, that will give you new knowledge, and that will enable you to better help the next person you pray for. The choice is yours to make—each time.

You must, at the same time, help those who are not healed when you pray for them—help them to not be discouraged. They will naturally be disappointed, often highly disappointed, but there is always hope. So encourage them to be prayed for again and again until their healing comes. It may be they have things to settle with the Lord, or many things to learn themselves, or need not necessarily to have their faith increased, but their unbelief decreased.

Whatever the reason, you must be prepared to continue helping those who are not instantly healed—or not healed at all. You must not abandon them to disappoint and discouragement. God has something spiritual for them even if they are not physically healed. If they have not found it themselves, you must help them to find what it is.

Prayed for 1,000 People

At a healing school that Beverlee and I attended, we heard a woman who ministers with her husband tell about the first person she ever laid hands on and prayed for healing. "He died within a week," she said. "I was shocked. I thought I had killed him."

"But that didn't stop me," she said. "Once I realized that there was healing in the Bible and Jesus said we could heal people in His name, I laid hands on every sick person that came within reach of my arms. I prayed for people in airports, in stores, in bathrooms, everyplace I could find someone who was sick. I was determined that people were going to start getting healed when I prayed for them, because Jesus said that's what would happen.

"I laid hands on people and laid hands on them and laid hands on them, and nobody got healed. So I would go back and read my Bible again, read everything it said about healing, and then I would read the stories of people like John G. Lake and Smith Wigglesworth and Maria Woodworth Etter and Kathryn Kuhlman and I would lay hands on even more people if I could find them.

"I probably laid hands on a thousand people before the first one got healed. And that first person was a man dying of cancer."

You Can Make a Difference

Remember the story of the wise man walking along the seashore? There was a strong wind and the waves were high and washing starfish onto the sand. In the distance, the man could see a little girl picking up the starfish and throwing them back into the ocean. He smiled graciously as he got closer to her and said, "Little girl, what are you doing?

"I'm saving the starfish," she said.

He laughed, amused at her childish way, and said, "Why, little girl, you can't possibly save all those starfish, the waves are too strong. What you're trying to do just won't make any difference."

The little girl looked at the wise man for a moment, as if thinking about what he said, and then picked up another starfish and threw it as far as she could into the water. Turning back to the wise man, she said in her childish way, "It makes a difference to that one."

Don't Be Afraid to Fail—Be Afraid Not to Try

Sometimes things in life are so tough and so uncertain that all you can do is pull the trigger and ride the bullet. Sometimes it will hit its mark, sometimes it will not. But no one becomes an expert at anything if they never try—

and the worse reason for never trying is being afraid to fail. Don't be like so many who do nothing, and yet think they would be a success if they did. As Aesop said, "It is easy to be brave from a safe distance."

Somewhere out there is a person who will live out their life sick and oppressed, or never get a chance to live out their life at all, if you give in to failure, if you quit trying, if you allow disappointment to become discouragement and defeat you. There is a meeting place in God's timing, a synchronicity in your life and the life of a person who needs your help—will you be there and be ready?

Two scriptures that God gave to others to help them, and that the Holy Spirit gives to us.

God has not given us a spirit of fear, but of power and of love and of a sound mind (2 Timothy 1:7).

"Do not be afraid of their faces, For I am with you to deliver you," *says the LORD* (Jeremiah 1:8).

TEN

Be Determined to Succeed

And He said to them, "Which of you shall have a friend, and go to him at midnight and say to him, 'Friend, lend me three loaves;' for a friend of mine has come to me on his journey, and I have nothing to set before him'; and he will answer from within and say, 'Do not trouble me; the door is now shut, and my children are with me in bed; I cannot rise and give to you'? "I say to you, though he will not rise and give to him because he is his friend, yet because of his persistence he will rise and give him as many as he needs (Luke 11: 5-8).

Now He was telling them a parable to show that at all times they ought to pray and not to lose heart, ...
(Luke 18:1, NASB).

"*I* was so hungry for the power of God it was all I could think about ... I would cry out to God for it as I went about my day ... more and more I wanted to be separated from the world and be holy and righteous ... I didn't care what that holy power would cost me ... I would pay the last penny ... nor did I care how many times I failed ... I would get up, dust myself off, and try again ... I was determined beyond anything earthly to get Holy Spirit power like Jesus and the Apostles had ... or die trying."

Doesn't that summarize the spirit, soul, and body attitude of John G. Lake, and his journey to spiritual power? It started with a desperate hunger, and all the attending things that developed from it, and continued into a determination to succeed that not all the natural laws of the universe, or all the forces of Satan himself, could hold back.

Indeed, that attitude of spirit, soul, and body applied to anything of earth or heaven will *always* succeed in obtaining its goal. It's a universal principle that cannot be denied. You can have anything of heaven or earth if you are determined enough, and are willing to pay the price and become and do whatever is necessary to obtain it.

The Son of God wanted the gift of eternal life for all those the Father gave Him from the beginning to the end of time (John 17:2). He was told the cost, what He must be and do, the price He must pay, and He walked the road of our redemption and paid the price for you and me (Acts 20:28, 1 Peter 1:18-19).

What if He had said He didn't care enough, the cost was too high, the journey too long and difficult—fraught with dangers, devils, failures, and pain? Where would you and I and millions of others be today? Still sitting in darkness, without hope and without God in the world—under the power and oppression of the forces of evil.

And if the apostles and the comparative handful of early Christians had not listened to Jesus, believed in Him, and believed Him when He told them that they would receive the Holy Spirit as their Comforter and Guide, and believed that He Himself would always be with them in all their spiritual journeys, we would still be in the same lost conditions.

Consider, then, what would have happened—or not happened—to the hundreds-of-thousands of the sick and oppressed in South Africa; Spokane, Washington; and Portland, Oregon, if John G. Lake had not taken his spiritual journey. Had not walked the road to spiritual power with all its dangers and difficulties. Had not looked at the lives of Jesus and the apostles, at the lives of those like Dorothea Trudel and Alexander Dowie and unknown numbers of others down through the grand healing history of the Church, and said to himself, "I can have the same spiritual power that they had, and in the name of Jesus Christ, the Son of the living God, I *shall* have it."

Now consider yourself.

You are hungry for the spiritual power to heal the sick and the oppressed, you now know what is required of you, and you are willing to be and do whatever is necessary to obtain it. So the only question that remains is whether you have the inner discipline and determination that you will need to sustain you for whatever length of time it takes.

Look, the discipline and determination that it takes to win a medal in the Olympics is the same discipline and determination that it takes to be a winner in the kingdom of God. The only difference is that for the Olympics the discipline and determination are focused upon the physical, and for the kingdom of God the discipline and determination are focused upon the spiritual. But it's the same principle for both. It's just as plain as that, there's nothing mysterious or mystical about it.

But even as out of the hundreds-of-thousands of athletes there are only a few who make it to the Olympic winner's circle, so there are only a few out of the millions of Christians who make it to the kingdom of God winner's circle. And although there are differences in natural ability, it's discipline and determination that make the biggest difference between winning and losing. Some have it, some don't. Some will, some won't. As it is for natural matters, so it is for spiritual matters. Even the apostle Paul compared the Christian life to running a race, and to winning and losing.

> *Do you not know that those who run in a race all run, but one receives the prize? Run in such a way that you may obtain it* (1 Corinthians 9:24).

And he spoke of himself as both having fought a good fight and run a good race.

> *I have fought the good fight, I have finished the race, I have kept the faith* (2 Timothy 4:7).

So it's easy to understand, easy to plainly see, that after all the reading, studying, and learning there is a fight to be fought and a race to be run in order to obtain the spiritual power that is needed to heal the sick and oppressed—and that the fight and the race demand discipline and determination to win. It is also clear from all that you have read in this book and the several others that you have read, that even after you have obtained spiritual power like John G. Lake and others had, there will be times when the only things that will make a difference between success and failure, even life and death, will be your discipline and your determination.

Letwaba's Determination

One day I sat talking to Tom Seymour in Los Angeles. I told him about the following incident in the life of Elias Letwaba, one of our native preachers in South Africa.

I went to Letwaba's house one day in the country, and his wife said, "He is not home. A little baby is hurt, and he is praying for it."

So I went over to the native hut where he was, got down on my knees, and crawled inside. I saw Letwaba kneeling in a corner by a child. I said, "Letwaba, it is me. What is the matter with the child?"

He told me the mother had been carrying it on her back in a blanket, as natives carry their children, and it fell out. He said, "I think it hurt its neck."

I examined the baby and saw that its neck was broken. It would turn from side to side like the neck of a doll. "Why, Letwaba, the baby's neck is broken!"

I did not have faith for a broken neck, but Letwaba did not know the difference. I saw that he did not understand. He discerned the spirit of doubt in my soul, and I said to myself, I am not going to interfere with his faith. He will just feel the doubt generated by all the old traditional things I have learned, so I will go outside.

I went to another hut and kept on praying. I lay down at 1 a.m. At 3 o'clock, Letwaba came in.

I said, "Well, Letwaba, how about the baby?"

He looked at me, so lovingly and sweetly, and said, "Why, brother, the baby is all well! Jesus do heal the baby."

I said, "The baby is well! Letwaba, take me to the baby at once."

So we went to the baby. I took the little thing on my arm and came out of the hut praying: "Lord, take every cursed thing out of my soul that keeps me from believing the Lord Jesus Christ."

As I related the incident to Mr. Seymour, he shouted, "Praise God, brother! That is not healing—it is life!"

Lake's Son Healed Once Instantly, Second Time by Lake's Determination

In 1913, I was in Chicago in a big meeting, when I received a telegram from the hospital in Detroit, saying, "Your son Otto is sick with typhoid fever. If you want to see him, come."

I rushed for a train, and when I arrived, I found him in a ward. I told the man in charge I would like a private room for him, so I could get a chance to pray for him. Well, God smote that thing in five minutes. I stayed with him for a couple of days until he was up and walking around.

He went along for four or five weeks, and one day to my surprise I got another telegram, telling me he had a relapse of typhoid. So I went back. This time there was no sunburst of God like the first time. Everything was as cold as steel, and my, I was so conscious of the power of the devil.

I could not pray audibly, but I sat down by his bed and shut my teeth, and I said in my soul, Now, Mr. Devil, go to it. You kill him if you can. And I sat there five days and nights. He did not get healing the second time instantly. It was healing by process—because of the fact that my soul took hold on God. I sat with my teeth shut, and I never left his bedside until it was done.

You may be healed like a sunburst of God today and tomorrow. The next week or month when you want healing, you may have to take it on the slow process. It will be the same for those to whom you minister. The action of God is not always the same, because the conditions are not always the same. Hold fast; be determined to succeed.

The Character of Jesus Christ

In this land, after our forefathers had signed the Declaration of Independence they pledged, "Our lives, our fortunes, and our sacred honor," then they went out and gave themselves to eight years of war in order to make it good.

When people make a declaration on principles, it is going to cost them something and it often costs them a great deal. After awhile the men in the old Revolutionary Army got where they did not have shoes on their feet, but in the depth of winter they tied straw and rags on their feet. They had stood by principles, they had lived by principles, they were ready to die by principles, and the British tracked them by the blood marks on the snow.

So Jesus Christ, in enlisting an army, put them under a kindred pledge with Himself. He pledged Christians on the same plane with Himself. Just as far as the Lord went, they went "even to the point of death" (Acts 17:28).

The real purpose of becoming a Christian is not to save yourself from hell or to be saved to go to heaven. It is to become a child of God with the character of Jesus Christ, to stand before men pledged unto the uttermost "even to the point of death" by refusing to sin, refusing to bow your head in shame, by refusing to give up. Preferring to die rather than dishonor the Son of God.

If the character of Jesus Christ has entered into you and into me, then it has made us like the Christ. It has made us like Him in purpose. It has made us like Him in fact. Bless God! His Spirit is imparted to us. Bless God for that same unquenchable fidelity, that same strength and determination that characterized the Son of God.

Union Between Christ and the Christian

There is a union between Christ and the Christian that is so deep, so pure, so sweet, so real that the very conditions of the human spirit are transmitted to His, and the conditions of the Christ's Spirit are transmitted to ours. It is because of the continuous inflow of the Spirit of Christ in our heart that we appreciate or realize His power and triumph. It lifts us above our surroundings and causes us to triumph anywhere and everywhere (Romans 8:37)

The Christian life is designed by God to be a life of splendid, holy triumph. That triumph is produced in us through the continuous inflow and abiding presence of the Spirit of the triumphant Christ. He brings into our nature the triumph that He enjoys. Indeed the mature Christian, having entered into that consciousness of overcoming through the Spirit of Christ, is privileged to transmit that same overcoming power and spirit to other lives, in and through the power of the Spirit of God.

That is why Christians who are joined with Christ live, move, and have their being in the same life and Spirit and are therefore reproductions of the Lord Jesus Christ. (Romans 17:28).

Dedication, Determination, and Death

During one of the periods of extreme necessity in our great work in South Africa, our finances were virtually reduced to nothing because of awful attacks upon us that affected our contributions from the United States. We had one hundred and twenty-five men plus women and children in the field, and I was anxious that there should be no letting down of the work we were then doing. I was praying that it would not be necessary to withdraw our workers who had labored and suffered to get the work established on the frontier.

Not being able to supply funds to those in the field, however, I deemed it the only wise thing to do to get them all together in a general conference, let them know what our conditions were, and let them decide what was to be our future action. By selling everything we could sell but bare necessities, we succeeded in bringing in those one hundred and twenty-five missionaries from the field for a council. I told them the existing conditions, and we sat down in the nighttime to decide what would be our future policy.

After a time, I was invited by the men to leave the room while they talked among themselves. After awhile they called me back in and said to me, "Brother Lake, we have arrived at a decision."

Old father Van der Wall spoke for the company. He said, "We have reached this conclusion. There is to be no withdrawal of anyone from any position. We feel that the time has come when your soul ought to be relieved of responsibility for us. We feel we have weighted your life long enough, but now, by the grace of God, we return to our stations to carry on our work. We live or die depending on God. We are going back if our wives die. We are going back if our families die. We are going back if we die ourselves. If we survive, we survive; but we are going back to our stations. This work will never be withdrawn. We have but one request: if we die, we want you to come and bury us. Now serve the communion of the Lord's Supper to us once more while we stand together."

As I took the cup, they arose and stood in a large circle. I took the bread and passed it. It went from hand to hand around the circle. When it came time to pass the wine, I took the cup in my hand, and with the usual statement that Jesus gave in the committal of Himself to God, "My blood in the New Testament." I passed it on and the next one, looking up to God, said also, "My blood in the New Testament." And so it passed from hand to hand clear around the circle.

Within a year, I buried twelve men and sixteen women and children. Every one of them might have lived if we could have supplied the ordinary essential things they ought to have received. But beloved, we had made our pledge to God. We had declared by the love of God in our souls and because of what Christ had done for us, that we would be true to Him, and that in the name of

Christ, His Gospel should be spread abroad as far as it was in our power to do.

Many have said that the Cross of Christ was not a heroic thing, but I want to tell you that the Cross of Jesus Christ has put more heroism in the souls of men and women than any other event in human history. Christians who realized the real high spirit of Jesus' holy sacrifice have lived and rejoiced and died believing in the living God and in the Christ of God whose blood cleansed their hearts from sin. They manifested to humanity that same measure of sacrifice and endured all that human beings could endure, and when endurance was no longer possible they passed on to be with God, leaving the world blessed through the evidence of a consecration deep and true and pure and good like the Son of God Himself.

We see the note that was in the soul of Paul, and which characterized his message, when he made that splendid declaration in Romans 1:16: "I am not ashamed of the gospel of Christ, for it is the power of God to salvation for everyone who believes, for the Jew first and also for the Greek."

Power of the Gospel of Healing

A woman came to our healing rooms, a stranger in Spokane. She said, "I have been praying for healing and asking God to show me where I could be healed. I heard of friends in Chicago who pray for the sick, and I visited them, but when I arrived the Spirit said, 'Not here.'"

She said, "I bought a ticket and was about to take a train back home, but as I sat in the station a little lady on crutches sat next to me and we started talking. During our conversation, I realized she was a Christian of a deep nature, rarely found. I told her my story.

"She said, 'Oh, I know where the Lord wants you to go. The Lord wants you to go to Spokane, Washington.'" (Three thousand miles from Chicago.)

She asked the woman if she knew anybody in Spokane and she replied, "Why yes, I know Mr. Lake. I used to nurse in his home years ago."

After listening to her story, I prayed for her and told her the thing to do was to come to the healing rooms for ministry every day until she was well. She said she would. This morning, I received a call on the telephone, and she said, "I am not coming up to the healing rooms."

I said, "Oh, is that the kind of individual you are? The one that comes once and gets nothing."

"No," she said, "I came once and got something and I do not need to come hack. I am healed and I am going home."

Desire and Determination

There is a call of faith in this church [Lake's Spokane church] that is reaching way out, far out, and in unaccountable ways. Away at the other end, the Spirit of God is revealing truth to this soul and that soul, and they are moving into this life and coming into unity with this church.

Is there a note of despair in your heart? Have you not attained the thing your soul covets? God will answer the call of your soul. You shall have your heart's desire. But before that call becomes answerable, it must be the paramount call of your being. It is when it becomes the paramount issue of the soul that the answer comes. Jesus knew. That is the reason He said, "Blessed are those who hunger and thirst for righteousness" (Matthew 5:6)

There is not a doubt about it. All the barriers of your nature will go down before the desire and determination of your soul. All the obstacles that ever were will disappear before the desire and determination of your soul. All the diseases that ever existed in your life will disappear before the desire and determination of your soul when that desire and determination become the one great purpose and prayer of your heart.

When the desire of your heart is intensified so that it absorbs all your energies, then the time of its fulfillment is not far away. When that desperate desire is combined with deep determination, the answer is certain to come. That is the desire and determination that brings the answer. It is creative desire, creative determination.

A woman testified in my hearing one day to this fact. She was going blind and had been told that there was no hope of saving her sight—no human remedy could do her any good. Someone opened to her, in a slight way, the possibility of seeing through the power of God. She was not very well taught, but she said, "Every day for four years I gave up two and one-half hours absolutely to expressing the desire of my soul for real sight." Not only expressing in words, but calling the power of God to her that would recreate in her the function of sight in her eyes and make her see clearly once more. At the end of four and a half years, she said, "My eyes are as well as they ever were."

This is the reward of persistence, of a desire and determination toward God. Your nature may have sent out just as deep a cry to God as my nature has and still is doing. Is your cry to God continuous? Gradually, as the forces of life concentrate themselves in line with your strong desire, the Spirit of God operating through your heart is being directed by that desire and concentrated on a particular line, intensifying every day because of the continuous desire and determination of your soul to possess what you need.

The effect of that concentration of the Spirit of God on your soul is that by the grace of God there is brought to your soul all the elements necessary to formulate and create and fulfill the desire and determination of your heart. And one day your soul awakes to discover that it has become the possessor of the desired object.

The Gift of Hunger

Oh, if I had one gift or one desire that I would bestow on you more than all others, I would bestow upon you the hunger for God.

"Blessed are those who hunger." Hunger is the best thing that ever came into a person's life. Hunger is hard to endure. It is the call of your nature for something that you do not possess. The thing that will satisfy the demands of your nature and the hunger of your soul is the call of your nature for the Spirit of life that will generate in you the abundant love of God.

Years ago, I was one of a family in which some member was an invalid in the house for thirty-two consecutive years. During that time, we buried four brothers and four sisters. A call arose in my nature to God for something to stop that tide of sickness and death. Man's medicine had utterly failed. One after another, the tombstones were raised. The call arose in my soul for something from God that would stem the tide and turn it backward.

Nothing else but healing could have come to my life, no other thing but the knowledge of it. God had to bring, from the furthest ends of Australia, Alexander Dowie, the man who brought to my soul the message of God and the manifestation of His power that satisfied my heart. And healing by the power of God became a fact to me.

Development of Our Soul

We live that our souls may grow. The development of your soul is the purpose of your existence. God

Almighty is trying to obtain some decent association for Himself By His grace He is endeavoring to have us grow up in His knowledge and likeness to that stature where, as sons of God, we will comprehend something of His love, of His nature, of His power, of His purpose, and be big enough to give back to God what a son should give to a great Father—the reverence, the love, the affection that comes from the understanding of the nobleness and greatness of His purpose.

Great Britain produced two marvelous statesmen, a father and his son. They are known in history as the old Pitt and the young Pitt. The young Pitt was as great a statesman as his father was. The son grew to that largeness when he caught the vision of his great father and his soul arose to it. When it did, he became his father's equal. As I walked through the House of Commons, I came across the statues of the old and young Pitt. I have forgotten the inscription at the bottom of the elder Pitt's statue, but at the base of the son's statue was these words, "My father, the greatest man I ever knew." Do you see the call of his soul for his father's largeness, for his father's nobility, for his father's strength and influence?

"Blessed are those who hunger." What are we hungering for, a little bit of God? Enough to take us through this old world where we will have the dry rot and be stunted and then squeeze into heaven? "Blessed are those who hunger" for the nature and power and love and understanding of God. Why? "They shall be filled." Bless God!

The Nature of God

Not long ago I stood before a large audience of the churchmen of the world. They said, "Through all your ministry there is one note. It is the call for power."

"Do you not think," they said, "it would be better if the Church was calling for holiness instead of power?"

I replied, "She will never obtain the one without the other. There is something larger than holiness. It is the nature of God."

The nature of God has many sides. From every angle that your soul approaches God, it reveals a new and different manifestation of Him: Love, beauty, tenderness, healing, power, might, wisdom, etc. So when you hunger and hunger, bless God, and lift your soul to God you bring God down to meet your desperate cry. Your spirit and the Spirit of God unite. The nature of God is reproduced in you as God purposed it should be. There are no sick people in God. There is no sickness in His nature.

There is an incident in the life of Jesus that is so marvelous. Jesus Christ demanded His right to heal a woman who was bound by Satan with a spirit of infirmity and was not satisfied until it was accomplished. Demon and church and creed and preacher went down before the call of the Son of God to assert His right to deliver that soul from sin and sickness (Luke 13:11-17) "Blessed are those who hunger . . . for they shall be filled."

The Spirit of God is Upon Us

We are living in a day and hour when the Spirit of God has come into the world afresh, when the consciousness of humanity is opening up to God in a manner it has never opened before. There is an awakening in the world from ocean to ocean, from pole to pole, as there never was before. And I believe that God Almighty's outpouring of the Spirit upon all flesh is at hand. And though we are receiving the drippings, and our own hearts are being warmed by the impulse of the Spirit, that day is not far distant when the flame of God will catch the souls of Christians and the Church of the latter day will close this era with a place of divine glory excelling that of the early Church.

This is according to the word from the Spirit of God: "If the former rain was abundant, shall not the latter rain be more abundant?" If the disciples without the train of Christian history behind them that you and I have, were able to enter into the divine consciousness and power of the Holy Spirit in such a way that they left a stamp upon all Christianity and the world, how much more shall men and women who have the advantage of 2,000 years of Christian record, enter into a divine consciousness that not even the apostles possessed!

John G. Lake's Consecration to God

Principle 1

All things earthly that I possess shall not be considered my own, but belonging to my heavenly Father, and shall be held in trust by me to be used and directed by the wisdom of the Spirit of God, as the law of love of men as Christ loved them may dictate.

If at anytime God should raise up men wiser than myself, I will gladly commit my all to their use and turn over all my possessions to them for distribution.

If at anytime in my life I should be engaged in any earthly business and should employ men to aid me in conducting it, I shall reward them justly and equally, comparing their own energy expended with my own after adding a sufficient amount to my own to cover all risk that may be involved in the operation of my business.

I shall consider my employees my equals with rights to the blessings of nature and life equal to my own. I shall not strive to elevate myself to a position of comfort above the rest of my employees and shall direct all my efforts to bring all mankind to an equal plane, where all enjoy the comforts of life and fellowship together.

Principle 2

I shall not cease to cry to God and implore Him to deliver mankind from the effects of sin so long as sin lasts, but shall cooperate with God in the redemption of mankind.

I will have seasons of prayer and fasting in behalf of mankind, weeping and bewailing their lost condition and imploring God to grant them repentance unto life as the Spirit of God may lead me.

Principle 3

I shall live my life in meekness, never defending my own personal rights, but shall leave all judgment in God who judges righteously and rewards all according to their works.

I shall not render evil for evil or railing for railing, but shall bless all and do good to enemies to return [good] for evil.

By God's grace I shall keep all hardness and harshness out of my life and actions, but shall be gentle and unassuming, not professing above what God has imported to me, nor lifting myself above my brethren.

Principle 4

I shall consider righteous acts as more necessary to life and happiness than food and drink, and not let myself be bribed or coerced into any unrighteous action for any earthly consideration.

Principle 5

By God's grace, I will always be merciful, forgiving those who have transgressed against me and endeavoring to correct the ills of humanity instead of merely punishing them for their sins.

Principle 6

I shall not harbor any impure thoughts in my mind, but shall endeavor to make my every act uplifting.

I shall regard my procreative organs sacred and holy and never use them for any purpose other than that which God created them for.

I shall regard the home as sacred and always guard my actions in the presence of the opposite sex, so as not to cause a man and his wife to break their vows to one another. I shall be chaste with the opposite sex who are married, considering them as sisters. I shall be careful not to cause them undue pain by playing on their affection.

Principle 7

I will always strive to be a peacemaker. First, by being peaceful myself and avoiding all unfruitful contentions and treating all with justice and regarding their rights and their free agency, never trying to force any to my point of view.

If I should offend anyone knowingly, I shall immediately apologize.

I will not scatter evil reports about any person and so try to defame their character, or repeat things that I am not certain of being true.

I will strive to remove the curse of strife among brethren by acting as a peacemaker.

Principle 8

I shall not become discouraged when I am persecuted on account of the righteousness mentioned above nor murmur on account of any suffering I undergo, but shall gladly give my life rather than depart from this high standard of life, rejoicing because I know I have a great reward in heaven.

I shall strive to make the above principles the ideal of all the world and give my life and energy to see mankind get the power from God to practice the same.

John G. Lake's Radio Lectures

Lake gave a series of twelve brief radio lectures in the summer of 1935. They were probably no more than ten minutes long, and were all titled, "Adventures in Religion." The first was given on June 24 and the last on August 22, just twenty-five days before he died. Here are his first and last radio lectures.

RADIO LECTURE 1 - JUNE 24, 1935

This is the first of a series of articles on the general subject of, "Adventures in Religion." I want to remind you for a few moments of some of the old mystics who were given glimpses into the unseen that it has not been the privilege of the ordinary man to understand.

ST. FRANCIS OF ASSISI (1181 – 1226)

The first and foremost was St. Francis of Assisi, whom the world has conceded to be one of the most Christ-like characters who has ever lived in the world.

ST. JOHN OF THE CROSS (1542 – 1591)

At a later period came St. John of the Cross, who for ten years seemed to live detached from the world. Today, he is discovered to be one of the most practical men.

MADAME JEANNE GUYON (1647 – 1717)

At a later period, Madam Guyon appeared on the scene, and most every library contains one of her books. The molding of her character was so amazing that it has caused much discussion in the religious world of our day. (See the Pure Gold Classic, *Madame Jeanne Guyon*, published by Bridge-Logos Publishers.)

JOHN WESLEY (1703 – 1791)

John Wesley, the founder of the Methodist church, records two hundred and forty cases of healing having taken place in his lifetime under his personal ministry. It's reported it included his horse, Dan. Dan became so lame on one of Wesley's preaching trips that he wasn't able to carry him further. Wesley got down and prayed by the roadside, and God instantly healed the horse.

CHARLES GRANDISON FINNEY (1792 – 1875)

We have only, however, to look over the records of our own land to see many others. Such men as Charles G. Finney, founder of Oberlin College, and its first president. He was a practicing lawyer. He was seized with a conviction for sin so pungent that he returned to the woods to pray, and the Spirit of the Lord came upon him so powerfully, so divinely and took such amazing possession of him, that he tells us he was compelled to cry out to God to cease lest he should die. His wonderful ministry in the land is so well known; his books so frequently found in our libraries, that it is not necessary to discuss him further. (See the Pure Gold Classic, *Power, Passion, & Prayer*, published by Bridge-Logos Publishers.)

DOROTHEA TRUDEL (1813 – 1862)

The modern teaching on divine healing received a new impetus through Dorothea Trudel, a factory worker in one of the German provinces. She was tubercular and was healed in answer to her own prayer of faith. The result was that eventually her work developed until ten thousand people were healed by the power of God. She was not a priest or a prophet, just a simple factory girl in the hands of God. The German government licensed her institution at Mannendorf. It is on the record to this day, the first Divine Healing Institute established in the modern world.

From that time on, the whole subject of healing began to break out here and there. Among the writers on the subject of healing, who are well known in the Christian church, are A. J. Gordon, Dr. A. B. Simpson of the Christian and Missionary Alliance, and Rev. Andrew Murray of South Africa. Andrew Murray's books are in every first-class Christian library.

JOHN ALEXANDER DOWIE (1847 – 1907)

On this list, I wish to mention one who is not usually mentioned so lovingly as others. He was a Scottish boy, educated in the University of Australia, John Alexander Dowie. His ministry was marked by the supernatural.

It is a matter of public record and one of the most astonishing facts that on one occasion, Dowie invited all persons who were healed under his ministry to attend a meeting at the auditorium in Chicago. Ten thousand people attended the meeting. At the appropriate moment they all arose and gave testimony to the fact that they were healed. Those who were not able to attend were asked to send in a card, three and a half inches square, telling of their healing. Five bushel baskets were filled with these cards, representing the testimony of 100,000 people. At the proper moment, these five bushel baskets of cards were spilled over the stage to emphasize the extent and power of God's ministry and blessing to the people.

HUDSON TAYLOR (1832 – 1905)

Again, I want to call your attention to another marvelous life, that of Hudson Taylor, founder of the China Inland Mission. To him the Lord came not only in personal presence, but also in prophecy concerning the future. It was Hudson Taylor who prophesied the great revival in Wales ten years before it came to pass, giving almost the very day on which it would begin, and its power and extent. All this came to pass just as he had outlined it, while he was in the heart of China.

WELSH REVIVAL (1904 – 1905)

The Welsh revival was one of the most remarkable revivals ever produced. It was apparently prayed out of heaven by a single little church whose lights were never extinguished for seven years. This indicates that if a portion of that congregation was continually in prayer to God, that God would send a revival. And thus, it came, the most astonishing and intensely powerful revival. In small churches which would hold perhaps 500 people, in one corner fifty people would be singing praises of God, thirty-five people would be down praying, another group would be praising God and testifying of His power.

It was not produced by evangelism, but it was the descent of the Spirit of God on the people. Conviction for sin was so powerful, people knelt in stores, in the factories and mines, in their homes, or wherever they were to give themselves to God. Sometimes while men were drinking in the public houses at the bar, they would cry out to God and give their hearts to Him.

CHARLES F. PARHAM (1873 - 1929)

Beginning with the Welsh revival, there was a movement of God that spread throughout the world. In our own land, we were particularly and wonderfully blessed by a movement that began in Topeka, Kansas, on New Year's Eve, 1900, at Bethel Bible College, which was in a castle-like mansion called Stone's Folly near present-day S.W. 18th and Stone under the ministry of Charles Parham.

AIMEE SEMPLE MCPHERSON (1890 – 1944)

As a result of that movement of God, there arose a phenomenal group of men and women. Aimee Semple McPherson was one. She was a young girl on a farm in Ontario, Canada. She attended a meeting by a young Irishman, Robert Semple, who was preaching under the anointing of the Holy Ghost. She became convicted of sin, opened her heart to God and found Him, and was baptized in the Holy Ghost. Finally they were married and went as missionaries to China, where he died of fever. She was left a widow, and soon with a newborn baby. Some friends provided the funds that brought her back to the United States. Later she formed the acquaintance of a fine young businessman, and decided to settle down and forget all her burning call to the Gospel. This she tried to do. Two children were born to them. And then one day God came to Aimee in a meeting at Berlin, Ontario, conducted by Rev. Hall. Her early ministry, for a period of about fifteen years surpassed everything that we have ever seen in any land since the days of the apostles. (A multitude was healed under her ministry.)

RAYMOND RICHIE (?)

Again, I want to call your attention to another unusual man, Raymond Ritchie, who belonged to Zion, Illinois. His father was mayor of Zion City at one time. This boy was tubercular. They did not seem to understand his difficulty. He had no ambition; he could not work like other boys. He was in a state of lassitude. Eventually he found God. We speak of finding God as the old Methodist Church spoke of being saved, getting religion, meaning one and the same thing. When a man confesses his sin and God comes into his heart and gives him the peace and consciousness of his salvation, he has found God.

Young Ritchie, after his salvation, was totally absorbed in prayer, and the family got sort of worried. The father finally told him he had to get to work and help earn his living. But some woman who understood the boy said, "I have a room you can have." Another said she would provide him with food to keep him alive.

The great war came on, and the epidemic of the flu followed, when people died by the thousands throughout this United States. He became stirred and began to pray for people and they were healed. The medical department presently took notice of it, and they sent him to pray for sick soldiers, and they were healed. He has continued in the ministry from then until now, and he has conducted some of the most wonderful healing meetings that have ever taken place.

CHARLES S. PRICE (1887 – 1947)

Another man God has marvelously blessed and used is Dr. Charles Price. He belongs to our own locality. Price used to live in Spokane. Dr. Price was baptized in the Holy Spirit at an Aimee Semple McPherson meeting. Right away, he began to manifest a most amazing ministry of healing. I attended one of his meetings at Vancouver, B.C. He had four audiences a day and 15,000 people in each, and people for a block around who could not get inside. All the churches in Vancouver, I think, united with him in that meeting. It was the most amazing meeting I ever saw. The sick people stood in groups of fifty and he would anoint them with oil according to the fifth chapter of James, and then pray for them. They were so overpowered by the Spirit they would fall to the floor, and a great number were healed. (See *The Real Faith for Healing*, published by Bridge-Logos Publishers.)

RADIO LECTURE 12 - AUGUST 22, 1935

I want to tell you the story of an unusual family. I am going to call this story, "Following the Trail of Jesus." A number of years ago I felt as if I wanted to do something out of the ordinary to call attention to the subject of divine healing. So I went to the newspapers and posted $500. Then I announced that if anyone who was sick or diseased would come to the Healing Rooms and be ministered to for thirty days, and if at the end of that time they were not substantially better or healed, they could have the $500.

SPIRITUALISM

Over at Monroe, Washington, was a man by the name of Paul Gering, who had been fooling around with spiritualism. That dear fellow was an open splendid man. He was a hard-working businessman. After he got to fooling with spiritualism, nobody could live with him. He was more like a raging lion than a human. He went all over the United

States seeking deliverance from all kinds of folks who were praying for the sick.

He read my announcement and became interested. He sent me a telegram, asking me to come to Monroe and put on a meeting and, of course, pray for him. He met Mrs. Lake and me at our hotel and drove us out to his home on the outskirts of the city. He walked into his home and stopped in the middle of the dining room and fell on his knees, saying, "Mr. Lake, I am waiting for you to pray for me that I may be delivered."

We laid hands on him and prayed, and bless God, the power began to go through him. He was completely delivered, the demons were cast out, and he was baptized in the Spirit. From that time on, hundreds of people have been saved and healed and baptized in the Holy Ghost under his ministry. Now he is a great wheat farmer in the Big Bend country.

Last night I spent the evening at his home and conducted a public service for his relatives and neighbors.

TRAIL OF JESUS IN THE GERING FAMILY

Just let me follow the trail of Jesus with you in that family for a few minutes. His sons were unsaved; his daughters were unsaved. One by one after the father's deliverance, the faith of God in his heart laid hold on God for his family. They became converted and baptized in the Spirit until his entire family, including his beloved wife, were saved and baptized in the Holy Ghost.

Mr. Gering had a brother, Joe, a hard fellow and a heavy drinker. He owned a farm down in the country. His wife was distressed, for she saw he was gradually losing his grip on his affairs and squandering his money, and they were getting into financial difficulty. She was a woman of prayer and was praying for him. Finally, one day he came to visit Paul Gering. Paul said, "Joe, I am going to Spokane to attend Mr. Lake's meeting. Come, and go with me."

We were conducting meetings in our tabernacle. When they came, we were in the prayer room. The meeting went through without anything unusual occurring, until we were practically ready to dismiss. This man, Joe Gering, was sitting on one of the back seats. A lady turned to me and asked, "Who is that man on the back seat?"

I said, "That is Paul Gering's brother."

She said, "The Lord told me to go and lay hands on him and pray, and he would be saved and baptized in the Holy Spirit."

I said, "Then you had better go and do it, sister."

She went back to him and engaged him in conversation and finally asked if she might pray with him. He said he had no objection to her praying for him. So she laid her hands on him and began to pray. As she did, the Spirit of God from heaven came down on him, and in a few minutes he yielded his heart to the Lord and prayed through until he got a real witness from heaven and began to rejoice in the Lord.

After he rejoiced for awhile, she said, "Now you ought to be baptized in the Holy Spirit." He knelt down again and began to pray, and after a few minutes, Joe Gering was baptized in the Holy Spirit. That man's soul was so full of rejoicing that he spent the entire night singing and praying and rejoicing. In a few days, he was out among the sinful and sick and getting folks saved and healed.

Here is another portion of the story. These men had a sister who lived at Palouse, Washington. She was unfortunately married to a very wicked man. She developed a tumor and her husband insisted on her being operated on. She tried to tell him that in their family the Lord always healed them. He would not listen. So they brought her to St. Luke's Hospital in Spokane and she was operated on. A dreadful infection developed, and they wired to the family that she was going to die, so the family began to gather here to see her. I knew nothing of these circumstances.

I was riding up Monroe Street one day when the Spirit of the Lord said, "Go to St. Luke's Hospital and pray for Paul Gering's sister. She is dying."

I went immediately and inquired at the office and was directed to her bedside. I laid my hands on her and began to pray, and the Spirit of the Lord came upon the woman, the infection was destroyed, and in ten minutes, she was sound asleep. The next day was on the highway to a blessed recovery. These are some of the things that take place when folks get in line with God.

Their old mother was a godly woman who lived at Palouse. She had been notified that her daughter was likely to die, and when she got the word she went into her closet, interceded with God, and prayed for the daughter's deliverance. I believe before God that when God spoke to me it was the answer to that mother's prayer. He sent help through me, and the Lord made her whole.

GERBER GIRL'S HEALING

One day, Mrs. Lake and I were present in a gathering of Christian people, where these Gering people were and some of their neighbors. A family by the name of Gerber had a girl seventeen or eighteen years old. She stood up with her back to us, and I remarked to Mrs. Lake, "Did you ever see such a perfect form? That girl would do for an artist's model." But when she turned around, I was shocked at her appearance. I never saw anyone so cross-eyed. She was a dreadful sight.

Later, I talked to the father, and he told me that surgeons would not undertake to straighten her eyes. They said it was impossible, and if they undertook it, she was likely to lose her eyesight. Presently, the young girl came over our way and I said, "Sit down, little woman, I want to talk to you."

After talking a few minutes, I stood up and laid my hands on her eyes. The Spirit of God came upon her and in three minute's time, those eyes were as straight as they were supposed to be. She is now married and has a beautiful home and lovely baby. Her eyes and heart are straight.

Lake's Healing Rooms Revived

When John G. Lake returned to America in 1913, he went to Spokane, Washington. There he rented a suite in the Rookery Building to pray for the sick. The suite was known as the Healing Rooms. Lake and his assistants, who were known as "healing technicians," prayed for as many as 200 sick people every day of the week and as often as necessary. Over a five-year period, there were 100,000 recorded and authenticated healings. So many were healed that Spokane was called by some "the healthiest city in the United States."

In 1997, God called Cal and Michelle Pierce from Redding, California, to Spokane. For twenty-five years Cal and Michelle had attended Bethel Assembly of God Church in Redding, where Cal served as a board member and elder. In 1996, Cal was powerfully touched by revival. At that time, God gave him a desperate hunger for all he could learn on healing, past revivals, and movements of the Holy Spirit.

After long hours of prayer and a 40-day fast, Cal heard God say in February of 1999, "There is a time to pray and a time to move." With that came a certainty that God wanted them to reopen Lake's Healing Rooms in Spokane. On July 22, 1999, the Healing Rooms were officially reopened. Since then their Healing Rooms Ministries has moved around the world, with nearly 400 Healing Rooms established in over 20 countries under the banner of the International Association of Healing Rooms.

Cal is Director and Michelle is Co-Director of Healing Rooms Ministries. They both travel extensively speaking at conferences throughout the United States, Canada, and overseas.

For information on training or healing, you can contact them via their web site at http://www.healingrooms.com, e-mail them at healing@healingrooms.com, call them at 509-456-0517, or write to them at 112 East First Avenue, Spokane, WA 99202. The web site also contains a listing of the location of Healing Rooms in each state and country and contact information.